# View From Here

To Tom

Warmest Regards

Neil Richardson

21/3/25

Neil Richardson

Shield Crest



ISBN: 978-1-915657-62-6

MMXXIV

A CIP catalogue record for this book
is available from the British Library.

Published by
ShieldCrest Publishing,
Boston, Lincolnshire,
PE20 3BT England
Tel: +44 (0) 333 8000 890
www.shieldcrest.co.uk

# Contents

# Introduction

Many years ago, at school, I wanted to do so many things. And that is how it ended up. I did many things, career-wise that is. I did not achieve some possible career choices such as bank manager, architect, or strip club manager, but I have been fortunate to see life from many angles having worked in the transport, railway, legal services and supply chain industries at almost every level.

My education was nothing to write home about: 1 GCSE and a smattering of CSEs. Education was not the biggest concern in my early upbringing when everyone expected working-class lads to work in the mining industry, certainly in this neck of the woods. Nevertheless, based on stories from family members who have done genealogy, it appears that there were some brainy and "well-to-do" people in my ancestry, so maybe I have been fortunate to inherit some intelligence from past generations (or maybe not!).

This introduction is not a story of my life, more a brief background on where some of this poetry came from. Each one of us is a mobile story: a collection of biological parts exposed to varying experiences, and this, in a nutshell, is who we are. It shapes how we view life and if and how we communicate our thoughts and feelings in everyday life. For me, I think I came into the world with a capacity to observe, study, wonder and ponder. I felt affinity with the sort of movies that made one think. All my life I felt it fascinating to observe and try to understand what was going on around me, what motivated and made people tick, and if and why any of it matters. I have worked in jobs with the minimum wage, I have been unemployed for a considerable time, I have been self-employed, and I have experienced long-term secure employment. I have had tough, gruelling jobs; I have had cushy jobs with superb pay. I have worked at the bottom right through to having been a director, mixing with extremely affluent people at the top of the pecking order. Each of these experiences helped the blinkers come off.

In terms of emotional trauma, whilst I cover emotions and emotional trauma in my works, I have been very lucky and had very few major traumas or upheavals compared to some. But experiences are all relative. From my perspective, both trivial and more turbulent experiences (of myself and others) have all impacted upon my world, so much so that I believe that I am able to see things from many angles in an empathetic way. Yet I still recognise, there was always an angry young man in there that may nowadays be more akin to a grumpy old man – it's work in progress on that front so I apologise if some of my work may appear cynical. All depictions of poetry are exaggerated to try and get the point across, so please recognise if you do not line up to the sentiments or politics of the poem, do not be put off, it is just one angle and it may purely be the devil's advocate at play within me. There is no right, there is no wrong. Morals and opinions portrayed are only to invoke the reader to question and ponder. Not to lecture or cajole others into accepting the "View From Here". I consider myself highly unpolitical, but I endeavour to be highly moralistic. Not morals based on the views of society or culture or linked to any agenda but my own in-built morality navigation system. This, of course, is a very subjective area.

In the arena of love, I have had my fair share of ups and downs. I have caused suffering to others and have suffered at the hands of others. Of course, this is just phraseology; I am completely aware that it is only us ourselves that ultimately can hurt us. Happiness is an inside job, yet we are quick to hang the burden of guilt on others or be only too willing to accept guilt for hurting others. But the hardship of loss, whether it be love or otherwise, is well understood.

I believe in the fact that the future and present are, in part at least, down to your own expectations. I am lucky in life. Even when misfortune arises, I look at it from a positive perspective and every seemingly negative event has much in it which augurs well for the future if you look for it. Hopefully, my poetry may reflect some of this philosophy whereby one should be grateful and not be fighting to be in control of everything, but rather let the universe or nature weave its magic. It is very hard to paddle upstream and one soon gets tired, but if you sit back and let the stream take you, you can enjoy the view and not have to commit unnecessary effort. There might be some rapids ahead but hey, what an exciting adventure.

So, just a few paragraphs about me are probably enough for readers to have a little insight. This collection of poetry was written over many periods in my life albeit there are some gaps when I just did not write poetry. I never intended to write a book or a collection, I just wrote what I wrote when I wanted to and there was no bigger picture about what I might one day do with this poetry.

So please enjoy this collection and whilst I recognise much of it may not resonate with you, I am sure that some will. Similarly, some of the poems no longer resonate with me, such is the passing of the years and the changes I have experienced in beliefs and outlook.

**Poem Intro**

When I was a child and teenager, I lived close to Worksop College, a public boarding school, and noticed the differences between these elite boys and my friends and I on the council estate. The "school bully" is analogous to the public-school pupils and the "you" is analogous to us working-class lot.

# Who Split on School Bully?

A tap on your shoulder, you look around;
A smash in the face, you hit the ground.
The inflictor leaves like a human King Kong,
Who split on school bully? You did him wrong.

For he is a highly intelligent high-class threat,
A sportsman, scholar and a teacher's pet.
A lady charmer with a silver cane,
Torturer, sadist, his pleasure is your pain.
He is OK with a life lived fully,
You shouldn't have split on… school bully.

With his jet-set parents, his posh-man talk,
His pointed nose and his sternly walk,
Now he is behind the belfry with a victim in view,
Who split on school bully? Yes it was you!
You've seen the kids he's beat, lying in the gully
You shouldn't have split on… school bully.

1979

## Unappreciated Landscape

There we were on the A887
Where a couple of roads deftly join,
With my wife who is asleep beside me
As we headed towards Loch Loyne.

She had been reading her book so quietly;
The reason she never looked out is not clear,
Because I so enjoyed this beauty unfettered
As I kept a lookout for Red Deer.

But we may as well have been in our back shed
Instead of these visually orgasmic scenic climbs.
She can read any night snuggled in bed,
Ye Gods man – not here that's a crime!

Now months later, on a train approaching Brigg,
Passing over the New River Tome,
Can you guess what my Mrs is doing?
Watching TV on her phone.

Over Candley Beck up the incline
Into Brigg Station we roll,
Past the former sidings now just wasteland
Which once housed wagons of coal.

I ask, "What is wrong with you lady?"
She politely utters, "Nothing at all."
I say, "But don't you enjoy the beautiful landscape?"
But I may as well talk to the wall.

I say, "You have no soul my dear"
As I stare out at the Lincolnshire Wold.
In isolation I revel in this wonder
As stations and hilltops unfold.
We pass through cuttings and embankments
Run parallel to telegraph poles and a dyke.
And while I wish she could share all my splendour,
I reluctantly accept that we are not alike.

02/10/21

## Sally from Hartlepool

In a PVC skirt on a pub stool,
In a village near Hartlepool
Perches Sally with painted pink lips
With black knee boots and cellulite hips.

She's talking to the Barman Stan
Whose shaven head makes him a man.
How she loves this hard-man look,
How she loves a good hard fuck.

It's a pretty village off the A19
With a Norman Church and Village Green
Where the last bus goes at 9:43
And up the hill you can see the sea.

Sally thinks while the Barman serves
"Is this here all that you deserve?"
"Always forever to be bereft?"
"Chatted up, kissed, fucked then left?"

On her way home the tears drop,
Home's a flat that is atop
A Rift House located One Stop Shop.
Sally craves and needs this pain to stop.

Next night the world just carries on;
The village pub is devoid of one
Soon to be forgotten by all but me;
A body is washed up from the North Sea.

{Based in the Village of Elwick}

c. 1998

**Poem Intro**

I used to holiday with my auntie in the Tamar Valley in Cornwall either going on the train with my sister or on my own. I was so struck at the contrast of where I lived and this other idyllic place. I loved it in Gunnislake.

## A Panoramic Contrast

Far from streets of houses,
Far from urban takeaways,
Far from a labyrinth of alleys,
And three lane motorways
Is where you find my world
Of fields, valleys and trees.
Ye Olde Cottage, Calstock Lane
The place I yearn to be.

Far from northern mining
Where every village has a pit,
And no cloud a silver lining
Where joy is counterfeit.
Far from a constant stream
Of days, afters and nights,
My idyllic place is the contrast
I dream of here at night.

But alas my friend, one thing
A holiday is all it can ever be,
For I doubt my means can ever bring
This place as a home to me.

1979

**Poem Intro**

In the late '70s and early '80s, arcades and many pubs had stand-alone "space machines". Sometimes like a big box-like giant slot machine, sometimes laid out in a table format with a screen facing upwards and controls sticking out of the table ends like table-football levers. I was addicted and used to go into town especially to play these things. My favourite was Galaxian, but I was pretty adept at Space Invaders and Asteroids too.

## Space Machines

In a pub making a high-pitched din
Is a table where you put money in.
So, get comfortably seated on the stool,
And make sure the spaceship has enough fuel.

The amateur plays his friend face to face,
Each destroying the enemy from outer space.
Tense and excited makes for a sweaty palm;
You play much better relaxed and calm.

"Hey, see that high score up there?"
Must've been Skywalker or Chewbacca bear.
Thought that I was good, shooting on a screen,
But there must have been a pro, playing this space machine.

The stool reserved for the Buck Rogers type,
One hand firing, the other ready on "Hype".
I feel like I'm in a film, on the orbit of Tatooine;
Doing well now, got five thousand, three hundred and seventeen.

Built in Japan and exported to the UK
Into arcades and pubs for us all to play.
2 x 10p takes you on a trip to deep space strife,
Don't matter if you die; you've got three lives.

But you can't live forever, no matter how good a shooter,
I mean, come on, you are playing a computer.
I'm in the Marquis pub and I am seventeen,
And I'm just addicted, to... Space Machines.

1980

## Cottam Station

This was Cottam Station,
This was the former line
Where trains to Lincoln Central
Always ran on time.

This was Cottam Siding
From where goods were sent,
And where the boat train passed them
And rumbled o'er the Trent.

Now a country-loving couple
Reside at the station house,
And the track that once was double
Is a driveway for the spouse.

Oh, rural gaslit Cottam
You were a homely place to men;
I wish you lived in these fast times
For I never knew you then.

1984

## What the Redundancy Notice Really Said

Dear Colleague, we regret to have to write this note
To hereby notify and tell
That by a managerial vote
You are redundant, for all's not well.

Condolences must be forthcoming,
It is not our fault for well you know.
But from our position we are not shunning
And thus, you have to go.

After the loyalty you have given us,
We think it more than fair
To explain to you in double Dutch
That technology made you spare.

We hate this ruthless thing we do,
But we feel this must be done.
So off you go to join the queue,
For our rivals must be won.

Jan 86

**Poem Intro**

This is about observations of an adolescent youth (me) at 23:20 on a Saturday night in Worksop in the late '70s.

## Last Thing Saturday Night

Safety doesn't mean a thing; fights happen over a chick.
Violence is all around and people being sick.
Walking straight is a problem as is focussing those eyes
Whilst showing off to someone and telling a pack of lies.
Sounds of voices singing in grunts, sounds good when full of booze.
Chants together wake the sleepers; no one around can snooze.
A flashing police car light
En route to another mass fight.
Control is totally lost
Last thing Saturday night.

A couple of PCs patrolling pass a group of giggling birds
In turn passing a load of likely lads using uncouth words.
Every car is flying along fuelled by petrol and alcohol drinks.
Hospital is full of patients; got the Saturday night jinx.
An atmosphere of chaos and totally mixed-up drunken folk
Who will not remember tomorrow, what they are doing now for a joke.
Here comes the Sunday morning nightmare, hangovers and a spike.
Paranoia is the order, last thing Saturday night.

Accusations fly like jets, insults like lightning bolts.
Moderation levels are at nil and lack of diplomacy a fault.
One minute an adversary, the next your "bestest" mate.
Behaviour patterns are evident that are normally left at the gate.
The nightclub serves the next venue, for those who can stand the pace
Unless there is a party somewhere, anywhere for a drinking place.
And sex is on the mind nearly as much as lager and beer.
The ugliest, fattest lasses attract, and I am in good cheer.

Wonder why lager goes in brown yet seems to come out white?
Only time it ever happens, last thing Saturday night.

14/12/80

# Modern Boss Man

More loyal to his troops than Captain Bligh,
More middle-of-the-road than a road's cat's eye,
More jokes in an hour than in Hi-De-Hi,
More flowery in nature than a '70s tie
Is the modern boss man.

A dedicated sixth sigma and teamwork fan,
Younger outlook in life than Peter Pan,
A better work ethic than "man and a van",
Interviews candidates in open plan
Does the modern boss man.

Does the morning conference on exercise bike,
Faces the day with Bluetooth and mic.
"Hello Boss." "No, call me Mike."
Says motivated workers will never strike
Does the modern boss man Mike.

Boss man's image is all rosy and bright,
A platform to set the world alight.
Target driven, KPI, customer delight,
Buzzwords in Mike's arsenal right?
But I say he can't see sense from shite
Can the modern boss man Mike.

Boss man oblivious of a bursting bubble,
Creditors want paying, the company's in trouble.
But this entrepreneur with designer stubble
Can't see his efforts are turning to rubble.

Thinking his critics should just wait and see
Each night going home in his X3.
But termination comes soon with a capital T
For those who work for Bossman PLC.
Fear not for Mike though, for his family tree
Ensures the Jeeves-like boss man soon will be
Running another company for a modest fee.
Modern boss man is the thing to be!

1990

**Poem Intro**

Back in the day when Mrs Thatcher was extolling the virtue of lower income folk buying their own council house, encouraging us to want more from life and invest, which at the time was supported by low interest rates, I was maybe over-suspicious. Was it a genuine desire for the government to modernise the land and make everyone in society more prosperous, or was it a very clever ruse to get working-class people into debt to prevent ongoing industrial action and afford less control to the minions? And was it to allow property investment opportunities when defaulters in mortgage payments would result in more property being available for sale by those with more money? Who knows for sure what the real motives were.

# The Right to Buy

Places, towns, counties, cities,
Alleyways, subways, streets and jitties.
Things change but people not so much.
We will always be fooled very much
Like bunnies caged and not let free,
Tales of woe for them and me.

From Penzance all the way to Wick
They say be entrepreneurial, greedy and quick.
Buy an education and stop being thick,
And work for the things you used to nick.
Invest in big houses, mortar and brick.
I warn you all that this is just a trick.

The promise of jam will only bring pain.
Buy your council house but who will gain?
You'll wish you had your time again
When the rich your property do reclaim.
So… people, you go on buying to the brink,
But realise that one day you'll sink.
From Yarmouth to Barmouth there is a link
To get us all in debt is what I think.

Circa 1982

**Poem Intro**

Just put together based on the advertising jingles of the era.

# Buy It 1980

Drinka pinta milka day,
Have a Mars for work and play,
Or be a man to send sharks away,
Because the lady loves Milk Tray.
Or why not drink the Pennine Way?
Beans means Heinz, or so they say.

Buy this, buy that, they say you ought to,
Opal Fruits to make your mouth water,
Gypsy by Berlei: plungingly daring,
Quality Street, made for sharing.
'80s marketing is getting a grip
While British Rail say have a good trip.
Why not have 1 cal' Pepsi Cola
Or wear sports gear made by Gola?
Kill those stains with biological Bold,
Wear these trousers: Brutus Gold.

Advertising is getting better lately,
Buy it all in 1980.

**Poem Intro**

Based on observations from a passing freight train at Templeborough Steel Works at Ickles, between Rotherham and Sheffield where the Magna Centre is now, which at night used to be an awe-inspiring sight. At the time there was talk of closing much of British Steel. Templeborough survived until fully closed in 1993

# Templeborough Steel Works 3am

Dead: there's no sign of life anywhere
Looking around myself, smelling the coke burnt air.
Sidings: find old wagons, rusty to the core.
River: the Don, stagnant, unclean, impure.
Lights: reflected back, commonly orange and white.
Smoke: belching up, into a smoggy night.
Cold: shivery, squally gusts into the dark.
Sounds: buffers banging and hum of electric arc.
Barriers: unmanned, found on internal roads.
Dumpers distantly moan. Slag, the dusty load.
Stockpile. Scrap and magnetic crane
Inert… until 06.30 comes again.
Coke ovens: like a Hades scene of hell and fire.
Fences, concrete posts and aptly placed barbed wire.
Cars, vans, condensation screens on steel,
Old huts, mesh, discarded cams and wheels.
Templeborough: 3am, I ponder how long will it be here?
Templeborough: 3am, soon to be extinct, I fear.

1980

**Poem Intro**

Back in the days when I was a single teenager and drinking heavily in the town (if you can call 3 to 4 pints of watered-down lager heavy drinking – I was never hardcore) on Friday or Saturday nights, I would often write poetry when I got home in a big, red A4-sized book which I still have. Most of these were absolute garbage and nonsense but "The Pub Door" survived. The pub is portrayed as a den of iniquity in this poem but the undercurrent here is that the pub represented a bit of me that I was unhappy about. Pubs back then, and I don't know if it's the case nowadays, sometimes used to have a brass plate above the door with the landlord's name, hence that reference in the poem, and if not, then I must have imagined they did!

# The Pub Door

There was the door, with handles of brass;
Scratches on the varnished wood near
Walls of nicotine and coloured glass
And on the floor spilled beer.

There I was, staring at this door
Sitting in the Queen's Head at half past eight.
There was a millimetre between floor and door
And I stared at this door 'til it was late.

There above the door were written words;
Blurry-eyed I read the Landlord's title.
Underneath this passed "turds and birds".
In uncouth and rude recital.

There below the door is where someone spat:
It was phlegm, green and thick
Right there upon the welcome mat,
And that's where I was sick.

There adjacent the wooden door
Were the functional wooden frames.
I vowed I won't walk through the pub door no more
Cos I know the pub door's aims!

1980

**Poem Intro**

Imagine, a small circle of friends from the same street aged between 14 and 18 in a council house having a party. Two girls: One of these is Sharon, the girlfriend of one of the mates. Just a typical teenage party at someone's house while their parents are out over Xmas. This poem dates back to probably the late '70s or early '80s.

# Remote Teenage Party

Spin the bottle Sharon, for games are a lot of fun,
My sex life is rather barren, I'm sixteen years plus one.
The two girls here tonight, my league they out of be
And Simon in whose home we're in is in a similar boat to me.
There are jokes ringing out, Paul puts puns to play;
We laugh at not funny things to pass the night away.
This party in the suburb, under just table lamp as light.
Actions speak louder than words with a Skol or beer Snakebite.
But what the devil does this mean, where are the origins of man?
Are we all original sin, would this party Catholics ban?
Aimlessly I muse, as Funky Town by Lipps Inc rings out,
Give in though I refuse, what the heck's this world about?

Cans open to the beat, the beat is pending doom
In the sweaty heat, in Simon Burton's living room.
Crisps in a glass bowl, peanuts in a dish,
It's Xmas time again, I need a New Year's wish.
The gospels and the bible, it has no interest to them.
Bethlehem, stables, bright star and the three wise men.
Forget Jesus sandals, tap foot in left foot brogue
To "Tainted Love" Barry. New Romantics are en vogue.

A suburban teenage party, everyone here is pissed;
I reflect in drunken confusion & know my time on earth is brisk.
Not that I am pessimistic, but as I age each passing year
I'll look back at these photos and of what is current here.
And when all here are dead and gone, who will ever know?
The answer of course is no one, once we're 6 feet below.

So, all the people in this world, the ones that ever knew
Of this remote party, these people are very few.
An event in an infinitesimal point in the vastness of time and space.
I record this remote teenage party because it really did take place.
And I want someone to read this, about a party in England North,
For what will they ever make of it when read a thousand years henceforth?

Circa 1981

**<u>Poem Intro</u>**

Just a FICTIONAL story about experiences in a nightclub in the early 80's.

# The Nightclub Experience

## *Part 1 – Setting the Scene*

Look at them, rosy, red cheeks,
The modern fashionable disco freaks,
Multi-coloured lasers and a dig-it beat,
Bodies writhing in the clammy drum-beatheat.
We got it all here, Yazoo to the Jackson Five,
Alcohol's flowing; so c'mon boogie boppers: jive!

Whoop whoop.

### ***Part 2 – The Plot***

I was a little put out, a cloudy pint pot near,
I went to the toilets and brought back my beer.
The bystanders watched they could see I was drunk
While their feet kept tapping to the rhythmic funk.
From the toilets back to the crazy dancefloor scene
Where I spoke to this chick who'd just turned eighteen.
I asked her for a dance, and she sighed, "OK!"
Then when she saw me dance, she said, "Go away!"
So, I retired to a corner, felt a little left out
When a bird approached drinking Jubilee Stout.
She said, "Can I sit here, cos I'm here on my own?"
I said, "Sure baby, this is a 'you and me' zone!"
She was a real dish, her dress was pink
And being the bloke, I went and bought her drink.
So off I went for a Bacardi and Coke
But when I returned she was with this bloke.
I said, "Hey you!", then he got up and glared,
I said, "Do you wanna drink?" cos I felt quite scared.
Well, he was six foot two and looking down
Said he'd like a Newcastle Brown!
Pinched my bird, bollocks, what a cheek
I walked away nodding but did not speak.
Didn't return to see him but I saw my mates
They weren't interested in me cos they all had dates.

So, I was feeling lonely; I nearly cried,
Drunkenly contemplating suicide.
But dreams of a nice lay are not dreams of a life
"Please God, I'm not asking for a wife."
All I want is some instant chick,
I need one tonight so gimme one quick.
So, as I was sort of praying, a girl with blonde hair
Came to terminate my despair.
As she passed she knocked my drink on my lap,
She said, "Soz", and then we started to chat.
Turned out she was lovely, pretty and free,
We had much in common, she was just like me.
We just hit it off, with not an awkward pause
And I loved her gruff, deep feminine voice.
Yes, I have to say, I could have found no wrong,
Looking back, the lust and passion were strong.
So, I asked if I could walk her home on this cold night
And without hesitation, she said, "Alright".

***Part 3 – The Twist***

So... I went to hers for coffee, plan was working to a tee
And then she dropped it on me, said, "I'm a TV."
But I'd already stripped to my final sock
By this time, I was already hard as a rock.
He said, "Don't worry, it'll be alright."
"Do you like your guys in stockings or tights?!"
Never thought a Tranny would be better than my Ex.
Advice: Turn on your TV if you want good sex!

***Part 4 – Conclusions***

The disco floor is where my lesson was learned
For it was not a sexy female that I yearned.
So, all you people out there, just keep an open mind
And you never know what joys you'll find!

01/03/80

**Poem Intro**

It was evident many years ago that towns were stretching further out into the countryside, the roads were getting busier, more roads were being built and pollution was an issue, as was waste and fly-tipping. All man-related things which impact on wildlife and nature.
References: Donnybrook Fair was a fair that was held in Donnybrook, Dublin, from the 13th century until the 1850s related to noise, drunkenness and rowdiness. Morel: a mushroom native to the UK with an earthy smell.

# The Indifferent Dell

In the whispering wood at the sound of church bell,
Night-time arrives to the smell of morel
Where the lingering branches twist into a bough
It's photosynthesis live and under "The Plough".

Nature's fragrant sensation now raptures the dell,
The hare is for hunting, the vixen is fell,
The vixen is hungry, the leveret her fuel,
Does nature need to be so eternally cruel?

Later when the sun rises due east,
Insomniac barn owls and other such beasts
Witness brightening sunlight and noise in the air
And cackles and calls like it's Donnybrook Fair.

Summer is arriving, the spring soon to pass,
So, it's blackbirds versus worms in cuckoo-spit grass,
And through treetop messages devoid of our words,
We hear mating cry calls from some proud singing birds.

But amidst this beauty and tranquility, yet
Vixens and blackbirds know not of the threat
Of green lands and scenery threatened by black,
Of mankind's tyranny and unthinkable acts.
For what animals know of our destructive powers?
To the trees, insects, birds and the flowers
Life just goes on, like the flowing of a brook,
Just like you read in a Beatrix Potter book.
Yet this world is in the balance by one species called man
Whose upright ape-type brain, does not give a damn.

So meanwhile the woodland just plays it by ear
Unaware of the devil, having no conscious fear.
With more elegant offspring to come forth next year
To live and let live?

1984

## Climatic Exaggerations

In a shop you can hear them say,
"Bloody weather, what a crap day".
Downbeat about a little rain,
Starting on about the climate again.

And for those who are short of the verbal gift,
A mention of snow and of a possible drift
Compensates nicely and starts a social chat;
Climatic exaggerations are where it's at!

If it rains heavily usually spreading from the west,
A state of emergency exaggerates best.
And when it's in the 80s but it's really nowt,
They all predict that there's gonna be a drought.
Mrs Bea Upperty walking her dog in the wood
Treads in a puddle and calls it a flood.
Then on comes the BBC Weather Man
Telling us all that we are in for a tan.
McCaskill's wrong, there are no sunny rays
Just a cloud and showers and some drizzly haze.

We have some annual snow: so, give three cheers
To those who say it's the worst winter in years.
Prophecy of climatic doom from would-be seers
Yet the snow isn't even fit for skiers.

Anyway, round here even if bad weather does come,
Matters not cos this place is already glum.
And snow makes our garden look as good as the best
Climatic exaggerations: life's embellishment fest!

1978

## Wherever You Go (Same Old...)

What a world wherever you go
Through the Atacama Desert or Saskatchewan snow
Over the tundra or under, cottonwood trees
Whether in Pyongyang or at the edge of the sea,
The buildings look varied, landscapes diverse,
But something is familiar where er' I traverse.
There are Subways of the long sandwich kind,
Irish Pubs, McDonald's and Please Give Way Signs
And black and white people, graveyards and a clink,
Hospitals, pharmacies, car parks and precincts.
Yet this be no SimCity and this be no game,
It's the same old, same old, same old, same.

What a world wherever you go
Up the Mississippi or through Scapa Flow.
You might be a hippie, you might dress to show,
But you are stereotypical wherever you may go.
Am I not different? I guess the answer is no.
It's the same old world wherever you go.

27/11/22

**Poem Intro**

Just an observational take on a nightclub experience in 1980.

## Another Nightclub

Drinks all around make for a prosperous till,
The dancing girls get a sweaty thrill,
Nearly all the girls here are on the pill,
And a good three quarters dressed to thrill.

For nightclub goers it is preferential
To wear trendy gear, in fact it is essential.
A clinging skirt is a valid credential
For a sex life open and not confidential.

The beat makes the bodies here sway about,
The bouncers are present to kick people out,
For trouble causers and the drunken louts
And the music is so loud you have to shout.

The DJ digs the groovy scene
The guys are all looking rather keen
On the fairer sex who dance obscene
And you never know just where they've been.

The disco floor looks energetic,
Full of vigour and ultra-athletic
And looks are everything so it's aesthetic
To have faces hidden in sleek cosmetic.

The bar attracts a fair-sized queue,
Some sleeves rolled up to show tattoos
Which revel in pride from all that booze
And all his life remains unmoved.

I wonder how the bouncers cope
In the zany world of the stroboscope?
A shy guy sits in a corner and quietly mopes
Cos with these girls he knows he has no hope.

But many of the guys have customised cars
Which are not parked all that far
To tempt the girl who is minus a bra
To come and be his back seat star.

So as wanton hands undo a fly
I wished the nightclub a final goodbye.
It's not quite hell but promise do I
To not visit here or hell to the day I die.

1980

**Poem Intro**

This one is based on feelings sat overlooking Sheffield on one of the many hills surrounding it on a dark, rainy night.

# Rain On A City

Lines and lines of brightness glaring,
Merging with the darkened sky,
Beaming in the cloud's direction
Which begrudged fly.

From this little viewpoint high up
On this little windswept hill,
Sheaths of grass they sweep before me
Whilst larger things stay still.

On parapets of brick-built bridges,
On works of forgers' steel and joiners' wood,
Rain falls and it is so damp and dooming,
So miserable that it feels good.

Water from the sky is pouring,
Bellowing down like a voice box speaking.
Dim words washing into muddy puddles
And through a creaky roof that's leaking
There amid the pattering noises
Resembling the noise of a wheel in motion
Analogous to that of a white human
Spreading on suntan lotion.
Or spreading out his arms forever
Seeking urban cleanliness.
But tonight, it goes on raining
Tears of lonely friendliness.

The raindrops drip and drainpipes drain,
Gutters are full and clouds hide planes.
This is a Sheffield cityscape in the rain
I love to feel this way again.
And feel the downcast downpour pour,
This is beauty to the core
On a night in 1984.

1984

**Poem Intro**

Coming back on a coach trip from Paris I wrote this poem travelling up the M1 between Cricklewood and Northampton just based on the nighttime landscape.

## Here And There

The pylons stand, they look grand
Through farmers' fields and country land
Where it's dark at night, not much light
Except the orange from left to right.
The shining stars, the white-eyed cars
Looks like a scene from a '50s sci-fi on Mars
As traffic sways on motorways,
A continual stream through night and day
Where local folk say it's no joke
Handing petitions to council blokes
While unused church nave whose outside graves
Are strewn by the wind-blown litter waves.
As a train passes and goes the soft wind blows,
Clouds form quickly then it snows
On double yellow lines and Z bend signs
Which guide people through these modern times
To detached homes in smokeless zones
With telegraph poles for telephones.
Connect a concrete box to a tower block
Over the Northampton Arm Canal and lock.
Clouds reflect the glare, from a bus I stare
To this place which is both here and there.

20/02/81

**Poem Intro**

This poem is based on going to work on an early morning shift circa 5 or 6am. Many newsagents opened at 5am and as for going to work on a bike, well, lots of people did in 1980. Not because it was a healthy lifestyle choice or because of the environment but the fact that many people lived more local to where they worked, and it was simply the easiest and most economical way. Calling at the shop for a paper was the done thing. There were no mobile phones to entertain you in any downtime in work back then. So, the observations are based on real experiences and the feelings of the drudgery of having to get up and go to work at that horrible time of day.

# Morning Inertia

Dawn is here and I am cold,
The icy winter has come & taken hold.
No sunny rays, short, dark days
And I have morning inertia.

Waking up I cumbersomely do
Open the curtains and then look through.
I put on a tie & give a sigh
That's morning inertia.

Men pass who all look alike
Off to work on their pushbikes.
No ivory towers for another 12 hours
That's morning inertia.

My body's weary, eyes they drop
As men call en route at the paper shop.
A quick "Hello" then "Got to go"
That's morning inertia.

1982

**Poem Intro**

Wrote coming over the Cat & Fiddle to Buxton and then over the hills to Bakewell on a coach trip.

## Wild Moors

You wild moors, you beautiful moors,
You haunt me when I to you do travel.
You monstrous things you always draw
With mysteries to unravel.

You wild moors, you big green hills,
I fall in love when e'er I see you.
Come summer breeze or winter chill
I hear the wind or cry of curlew.

You massive moors, cloud searching land
With purple heather and fallow deer,
I know for sure my ancestors and
My kindreds lived and hunted here.

Oh, wild moors, you beautiful moors
Unravel the mysteries I do strive,
But secrets to be held forever more
Learn not while I'm alive.

Your valleys of trees and rocky brooks,
Your plateau pools and calming nooks,
Your forever alluring siren like moors,
You're my first love: I am always yours.

c. 1985

# Purgatory

This other tedious tiresome task
Of living a life and then to ask
Of God I enquire "What have I got?"
"Deprivation and barbed wire?"

To Gabriel, lest he listen on
Unto my morbid chuntering song,
Refurbish plush my death's desire
For green and peaceful state.

Because Peter's gate doth lure and call
Eventually for one and all
Yet ask me how I really know
Do I know? I haven't been

And if I should go I would not tell
If there is heaven and there is hell.
I would sit and smile on man's ideals
Of Eden's charms.

1984

# To Be Fourteen

To be a girl so young and green
Who strives to be a beauty queen
And look grown up when she is seen:
She hates the fact that she is fourteen.

She has a desire to attract a stud
To complete her ripening womanhood
With lipstick lips the colour of blood
To make her feel grown up and good.

She craves for sex to her child's side woe;
A prurient urge to set a flame aglow.
Her needs mean guilt: she feels low,
Is she woman or girl? She does not know.

She sees older girls all beau and chic,
Confusingly applicable to what she seeks
And resents her age with a fervent pique:
She is fourteen and feels a freak.

Her mixed desires are very obscure;
She is innocent but she is not pure
As her wanton digits heave and paw
To thoughts and acts deemed so impure.

Hiding a child's face with a makeup screen
And a uniform including tight-fit jeans,
She is learning what adolescence means:
She hates the fact that she is fourteen.

1984

**Poem Intro**

Travelling from Manchester to Sheffield on a train sat opposite a young woman of the same age. We keep finding ourselves looking at each other in the reflections of the window of the travelling train at night.

## Romance On A Night Express

Winter scenes are bare and chilling
When passing over an iron way,
Staring into dark reflecting
Eyes that quickly look away.

These eyes meet and clasp together
Like fate was urging something on,
But neither dare commence in talking
To spurn a romance on.

Over joints of silent whispers
Through the doubts that we will not bind,
Should a chance with zest be taken
To befriend a lonely mind?

Through rural bridges streaks the metal
Through Victorian tunnels with ash in,
Past blazing lights that are exempting
A burning unknown passion.

1984

# Listen

Listen to the nation, listen with intent,
Listen hard to the endless din.
Many have nothing to say but say a lot
So where do I begin?

Listen to the small talk, listen to the chat
About a neighbour's sister's friend;
A soap opera in local gossip columns
With pages to amend.

Listen to the media, listen to the press
That speak the truth and tell no lies.
But deception bends truth I surely guess
Brainwashing received through eyes.

Listen to the poets, listen to the bards
With their nuance and turns of phrase
That paint non-current pictures to people
Who prefer the hi-tech age.

Listen to the churches, listen to their bells
(Which I love) In praise of our dear Lord.
Confusing congregations of double standards
And the prophets go on ignored.

Listen to the intestine, listen to the food
That breaks right down to energy and shit.
Fast food, salt, sugar and crap
That's making us more unfit.

Listen to the whole wide world, listen USA,
Hear trendy imported language spread
What's cool is not cold and gay is not happy,
And sleeping together is not sharing a bed.

Listen to the voices, listen to the voice,
Cries echoing into empty space
Of a happy life forever yearned for
Listen to the human race.

1983

# Traffic etc

Stress with strain now flows in three lanes;
Pink sweaty fingers grip the wheel
In the ideal world where motor tax reigns,
As profit from people's "laze mobiles".

These are times of speed and haste
When progress is at stake.
We inhale carbon monoxide waste
And grouse about a headache.

The do-gooders say "Oh my gosh
Road deaths are now alarming".
In the neighbourhood where it's rather posh
"We'll bring in traffic calming".

Let joy-riders ride in council confines
In streets where the slums are situated.
Let's make some profits in handing out fines
While crime continues unabated.

We average 52 minutes to and from work
Every day of our working lives.
It's an average which many cannot shirk
And many more have a longer drive.

Old ladies tell hubbies to slow down a little;
Young men have testosteronic need.
The roads have made our tempers more brittle:
Road rage with road noise and speed.

Road works are on and the contractors in.
Holes are dug: cue temporary lights;
Lines besmirch our planet earth's skin
That weave like snakes at night;
And rise the gases into the ozone.
There's red signals at traffic lights
Will the world become a no-go zone?
And is the end in sight?

1984

## Don Valley's Final Hour

I no longer smell that coking smell
And the landscape now is bland.
An example is a factory shell
Perched on a piece of wasteland.

I no longer hear the hum or drone
Of steelworks along the Don.
All I hear is people moan
About where their future's gone

Those redundant - they have fear
Regards their vulnerable position.
They're cutting down on intake of beer
And seeing industrial demolition.

Sheffield thy greatness gone
It does seem such a pity.
So bleakness reflects back from the Don
On a disillusioned city.

Some blame the city council rates,
Some blame the union power.
Some blame the government or the state,
For Don Valley's final hour!

# LS Lowry's Lake

Inspired by LS Lowry's "Lake",
I wonder if he knew when painting
That pollution was so grave and tainting.
I wonder if he felt inspired
And knew earth's fate was so closely wired.
Whatever! His use of art was a gift acquired
And I'm inspired by LS Lowry's "Lake".

This image leaves me pessimistic
That mankind is so sadistic
That any hope for us is really dashed.
That human development cannot last
This is not an image of the working class
Or representation of us en masse.
And pitiful is such dourness pictorial
"The Lake" could stand as our memorial
And I'm inspired by LS Lowry's "Lake".

Inspired by LS Lowry's "Lake",
A whirlpool of sheer sensation
By a mind of extraordinary imagination.
This is true art and its' validation.
I just stare numb in admiration
I relate to LS Lowry's "Lake".

c 1985

# Morale

Morale: What is this thing called morale?
Is it comradeship with your cronies?
Is it a beautiful thing like Adonis?
Morale: What is this thing called morale?

It appears that people don't care
Moreover they seem to despair.
For when the workmates have lunch
They negatively meet in a bunch
And complain that the workplace ain't fair.

It appears people do not get a thrill
When their job satisfaction is nil.
When having no career plans
And know that management can
Discard their positions at will.

It seems that people do not work so hard
When incentives and interest are barred.
For the barons of fate
Run this business-like state
And are holding all the trump cards.

c 1985

They can send out a P45 if they want to
Sack anyone with no hoops to jump through.
So, work hard and don't ask
Carry out all of your tasks
Though they won't think any better about you.

Morale, what is this thing called morale?
Is it the incompetence and bosses' bad planning?
Stemmed from a fear of over-manning?
So what is the causation?
That surely hinders this nation?
Morale, what is this thing called morale?

Feb 1986

## Ignorance of Futility

The mind migrated, it had contemplated
Vast space integrated but at a loss
To explain micro against the size of the cosmos.
The mind's situation was like a terminal station
Devoid of motivation as all seemed nil
Except for love, no rationale or thrill.

The mind calculated how other minds over-rated
Their role falsely inflated, so infinitesimally small
Just so small. Has no significance at all.
Realisation was the mind's shortfall.

1986

## Love Avoided

I love but they hurt, I bleed when they flirt,
I fear the bond, they always respond
Initially fond, longer term wronged.

I love, I want to love more
But few are true to the core
Some love 'love' and what it stands for
But don't love you, but say they adore.
I don't trust love, I don't trust me,
I don't trust them, so I stay free.
A puzzle to figure I oft wonder why
How deep I want love but pass it all by.

2008

# The Organisation

Like an organism it thinks for itself,
A collection of particles working for wealth,
With a few at the top with the ultimate say
Moulding and shaping each working day.
Divisions apparent in pavilions of power,
Games being played each political hour,
Careerists are smiling and ask if you're OK
And then put in the knife and just walk away.

The internal strife, the external PR,
The smart business exec and his big German car
Contrast to the pawns who are means to an end
To which rules apply and no one must bend.

The bullshit emitted from meetings on high
Is as sick as Chairman's large dayglo tie,
There's a young middle manager waiting for a fall
Cos he said what he thought, and he dared to have balls.

Employees suffer from boardroom cop-outs
Of talented people in business there is a drought.
The Directors may moan, they may blame, they may shout
But corruption and greed prevail, of that there's no doubt.

1996

# Road Rage

Who can understand this young man, in a builder's van
Flexing his muscles and showing us his tan?
From behind his shades he shouts tirades
To two mature women he dubs "fucking old maids".

Who can apprehend this seemingly developing trend?
An Evel Knievel businessman screeches round a bend.
Like a lager lout except he's smartly turned out,
Another Jekyll and Hyde of which there's many about.

Even an old chap whose dad fought the Japs,
In his Triumph Acclaim, wearing his old grey flat cap
Is seeing red shaking his fist and his head
Giving a one-armed salute to the car ahead.

Crossing a double white line spells danger and a fine
But millions do it to save seconds in time.
In a rush to overtake she pulls a dangerous stunt
Swerving violently to avoid a head-on shunt.
The fellow now behind does not take this too kind,
Brain slips into red, and he has revenge on his mind.
He puts up a chase, so she ups her pace
And both become embroiled in a mindless race.

So, if other drivers misbehave or act overly brave,
Don't shout or rave, cuss, don't even wave.
Act your age, be sage, avoid road rage,
Be safe and think, sod em… it's their grave!

01/09/97

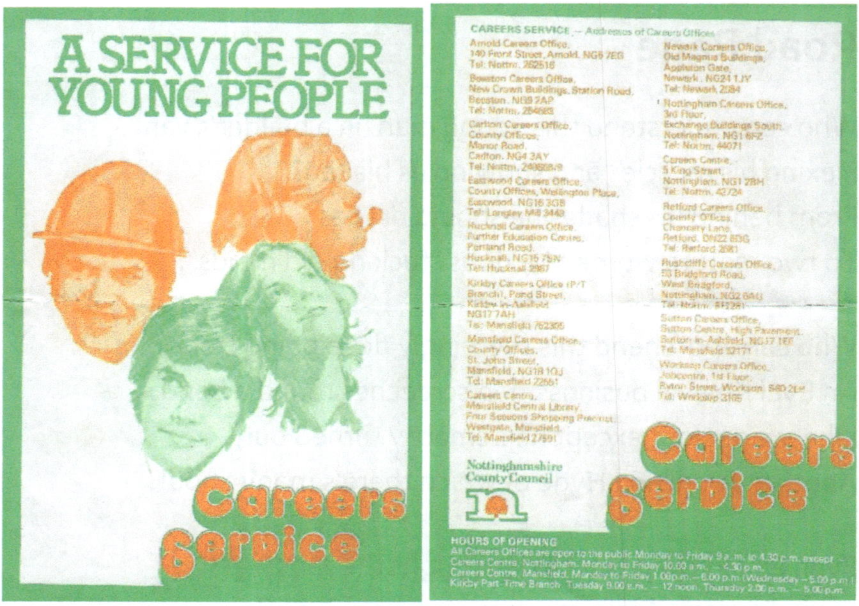


**Poem Intro**

My local colliery was Manton Pit where my dad worked, and it was within view and earshot of my former home. When this was written, there was a furious advertising campaign by the National Coal Board to bring in new recruits into mining coal with promises of long-term futures and great salaries. There were beer mats in local pubs saying things like "There's Money & Mates in mining". This was written as a type of barn dance song incorporating a bit of local accent and mimicking the irony of the upbeat advertising campaign at a time when many pits were starting to close.

## The Manton Pit Shuffle

Grab your partners by the knee
Come on coalies, dance wi' me
Dig that coal rayt out the ground
Wi' helmet on dance round 'n' round

Come on get your pit boots out
So it's eee by gum when coal's dug out
Manton Pit Shuffle, it's a rayt bloody treat
Enjoy ya dance in steel-capped feet

Round 'n' round on a Manton day
Get ya sen down to dig out rock 'n' clay
Bop to the boogie and smell for gas
As you dance to another face to blast.

Right now everyone's up that shaft
Dance even more but don't get daft
Thank them stars you're safe and up
Do the Manton Pit Shuffle and raise ya cup.

1979

# The Wedding

Two people throwing away their lives,
Neighbours watch as taxi cars arrive,
Two taxis gone, one more to go:
Here comes the bride, pure as snow (I don't think so!).

The church bit came, then it went,
They were married, heavenly hell-bent
To naively honour love and obey,
Yeah right-o, so... anyway...

To the reception there's a toast in place,
Groom's trying to put a name to a face:
"How do I know him and who's that girl?"
As he dishes out sherry, to Cherry and Shirl.
Meeting all, shaking hands and/or kiss,
Many tell him that married life is bliss.
"Oh, if only" – thinks his dad's best mate
Holding a buffet-fuelled bended paper plate.

The bride's dad bangs on the table and declares a toast,
Thanks the groom and says he is the most
Incredible guy, come on... you know it's a lie,
Only yesterday he was slagging off the poor guy.
More boring speeches 'til 6 o'clock
The bar opens hence and to it we flock..
Better still the disco comes to life
And we have the first dances of man and wife.
But I was still sober, so I didn't jive
Thought the dreary place would never be alive.

But the ale soon reached my sensible parts
And got me up dancing like a fart.
Still dressed in suit, collar and tie
Dancing with anyone who passed by.
I was well squiffy by half past 8
And the beer kept flowing 'til it was late.

They played Disco Duck & The Birdy Song,
With booze, cheesy songs can do no wrong.
I didn't know the moves, thought it did not matter,
But my moves made the happy dance-floor scatter.
I was ushered away by builders Terry & John
Who told me "No more drinks, not even one!"

Me, I fancied this lass she was not keen
And gestured me in a manner obscene.
Her fella looked like a right limp wrist
Until I felt the end of his fist.

I hate weddings and I will marry not
A happy single life is what I've got.
For no woman can have enough allure
To get me to bloody marry her.
My only vow I will ever make
Is I'll never be married and no mistake!

1981

## Prior To Christmas

Prior to Christmas, exciting times,
Kids in eager expectation smile.
Relations coming from many a mile,
Some youths on the street erstwhile.
Contemplate a burglary;
A man at a work's party lies
And contemplates buggery.

The dog in its basket sits,
Not aware that Xmas exists.
But ever since being a pup
Good vibes of course it can pick up.
Master says "Boy you've a present coming"
While Jingle Bells' he's happily humming
Like the dog understands?

The weatherman speculates
On white Christmas probabilities,
On temperature possibilities,
They always do.
He says "Take care"
Like he really cares?
Prior to Christmas.

My faith in God may be in doubt,
A hypocrite I hear some shout,
But even I can like this time,
Time of cheer and pantomime.
The Holly and the Ivy climb
Into my cheering soul
At this time prior to Christmas.

Date unknown

## Self Thoughts Of An Unconfident Female

***{An unconfident woman thinking}***
I can't flirt,
A fat little squirt
With a tart's skirt
And a man's shirt,
Full of pain and hurt.

I'm so plump
With saggy rump,
An unsexual lump
And no cards to trump,
Only the joker in my pack.

I want to play the tease
But with thighs like these?
Double chin and belly crease
Ugliness worse than a disease.
No love, no cure, no birds and bees.
Can I ever come to own or lease?
Send a lover please, I'm on my knees,
My search for love will never cease.

***{A man now interjects}***
Please weeping girl do not be so vexed
For many men are very highly sexed.
Many fish in sea diversely blessed
So come dearest girl and bear your breast.
Accept the first man (me) to do the rest,
And if you do not like the way you're dressed
Remove your knicks, remove your vest,
And let us have a raunchy fest.
Say "He Who Dares" and let's head west,
Trust me..."I am not like the rest".

***{Narrator}***
Oh, pity please this poor lass
For she's not dumb, she's not crass.
She is one of many in a pack or mass.
In a lower self-esteem masterclass,
I really do hope that she does not pass.

Date unknown

## Last Day On The Footplate

My last day on the footplate,
Maybe one day I will rue
On a late October Friday
Moving on to something new.

8 ½ years of service
In the loco cab.
It already seems a lifetime
And rarely dull or drab.

I have often found it tiring
And sometimes quite a strain,
And a fair share of exciting
Working on a train.

Ungodly shifts makes one unwell
Through countryside passed in haste.
But this job has a certain spell
And you know if you've had a taste.

My last day on the footplate
A day that I will mourn.
Is it a decision I will come to hate
No longer starting work at dawn?

I can't express (now there's a pun!)
That sadness cuts me like an axe.
About to leave on a local run
From York Yard North to Drax.

York Yard North at nighttime
For the last time I depart
With a coal train and a job
That I loved with all my heart.

Oct 1987

# My Old Poems

Brilliance is only found in those so blessed
With artistic talent above the rest.
As I look back to a past of verse,
I read my poems; man they sound worse
Than they once read.

I read them, chuckle, often laugh,
Some were so cheesy, poor or naff,
So full of naivety and now that I am older
I think I had a chip once on my shoulder,
I hope it's gone now.

Being candid and honest, regarding a former era,
Alpha waves strong and views held dearer,
But ability to transfer feelings onto paper,
I was a foolscap landscape foolish waster.

And, not surprisingly, I have to add
I was sometimes rowdy, bit of a lad,
After drinking pints on a Friday night
I'd come home after and poetry write.
But alas I seemed to always find
Any words to use so long it rhymed.
So "truth" was lost, squandered away
Not conveying the thoughts I wished to say.

Now the poems flow out better, I will admit
But inspiration that drives them has since quit.
So, bring me alpha waves please, and not frustration
And give me access to my imagination.

Now older I offer the chance to fulfil
The option of good poems written with skill.
I want consistent, flowing, nuance, grace,
Dynamic, touching, rhythmic in pace.
I want to touch people to look within,
And if not self-aware then at least begin
A journey where they can really win
And escape from the crap that lies within.

My Old Poems, times passed them by
Except in the Akashic up in the sky.
Most of my Old Poems ended up in the bin
But it does not matter, it is no sin.
It is what it is, do not search for why
Time will pass true; we all will die.
It is what it is, do not search for why
Just love and live and learn and fly.

07/08/92

# The Big Day

It's the big day, it's time to get ready,
Time to hide your fat and put a corset round your belly,
Time to don your stockings and garter up your thigh,
Time to get nervous, and not to doubt your guy.

The limo is arriving, the suits are getting out,
Your dad is on his 100th fag, then he has to shout,
"Come on duck, get your fat arse into gear"
"Bleedin' taxi is outside" then has another swig of beer.

The car is driven like a hearse, by 70-year-old cabbie
And you are not Princess Anne going to Westminster Abbey
Your dad is not Prince Philip, to whom you nervously engage in chat,
(Your dad that is not Philip) who remarks that you look fat.

Moving on, down the aisle, they sing "Here Comes the Bride",
You smirk from ear to ear as they look back at you inside,
Then the groom he turns, does he see the beauty on show?
No, he's clocked your best friend, sat in the second row.

The vicar seems a nice chap with a dialect-less voice,
Praises the congregation, then asks us to rejoice,
Your Uncle Keith, thinks he's Bing, so begins to croon,
Aunt Mabel she is wailing, like a banshee out of tune.
A right shower of musical shit, like an amateur gospel choir,
Weddings are just not my scene, bring on a funeral pyre.

The ring comes out the pocket, of the ale house Cisco Kid,
Not a Western hero, just a greasy bloke called Sid,
Who agreed at short notice, to act as the Best Man,
When the other one stayed in to watch Man Utd v West Ham.

We all go outside for photos, by a budget snapshot guy,
Who doubles as Marty Feldman, in his dickie bow tie,
Families pushed together, in a manner rather rude,
Not a great idea, considering their long- standing feud.

Wedding bells, public stare, soon it's time to go,
You trip on your dress, while confetti falls like snow,
It's not really confetti as you discover later in the car,
A piece falls from your hair, it's some ripped-up Daily Star.

Sherry, buffet, disco, follow on like cards in pack
On to a honeymoon in Costa Brava,
and then he gets you in the sack.
All is magic, all is love, as you do the dirty deed,
All to change in 9 months time, when there's another mouth to feed.

1995

## Young Finance Manager

Young and aspiring
Not old and retiring
Not shy
Very sly
Forever analysing.

Results received routinely
Checked so meanly
Does it balance out?
If not shout
Promotion sought very keenly.

Treads on toes
Looks down nose
Whizzy adder
Climbing ladder
Up he goes.

Jungle Law is there for all to see, he is like a monkey in this farce,
But the more a monkey climbs a tree, the more it shows its arse!

circa late 1990's

## Plane Crash Premonition

I had a premonition
I dreamed I died today.
I went white at check-in
On my way to pass away.

With a trolley and some cases
Walking feeling trapped.
Realising where I was heading
Departure lounge – how apt!

I had a premonition
I was shitting bricks.
Yet I made the decision
I had to face up to it

I had a premonition
I believed I would die today.
But all I got was a headache
As the Boeing went on its way!

c. 1995

# My True Love Does Not Exist

Wake silent from slumber in soft white linen
Next and close to one who is miles apart.
Will my drifting from this woman e'er be forgiven
As it stirs from the pureness of my heart?

Love should be total, consuming, pervading
Through every pore and through every hour.
But this love ebbed, and thoughts are invading
That the cream of my dreams has turned sour.

I drift to thoughts of my ideal lover
Yet pinching myself that loyal I should be.
Cheating in mind with a hypothetical other
Half feeling guilt, half in glee.

I embroil myself in not quite hallucination
Yet at the moment sometimes I never want to wake.
I want to know if the power of love consummation
Is here on this earth for to take.

The current non-existence of this mere mortal beauty
Bothers me not as much as the broken heart feels pain.
For being loyal to one is a moral bound duty
And prevents a dream girl for me to attain.

30th May 2000

**Poem Intro**

Following a visit to Rock in Cornwall and walk along the sea dunes and across the golf course to St. Edonoc church near Trebetherick, I came across the grave containing the ashes of Fleur Lombard in the cemetery there: the first British female fire fighter who lost her life in course of duty. The fire she died in was an arson attack on a supermarket started by Martin Brody in Bristol who escaped a life sentence and who was sentenced to 7 and a half years. The church is most unusual, rural and atmospheric and the thought of the events and this setting, inspired the poem.

# Reflections at St. Edonoc's Graveyard
## 2001

I met Fleur Lombard near Rock

On a windy afternoon

At St. Edonoc

Where the only flock

Were golfers & gulls

But none so noisier than

The wails of the Ocean wind

And none so eerie than

The way that Cody grinned.

# Chameleon Man

Chameleon man, changing colours to suit,
Only discernible to Kojak or Klute,
Overalls or business suit,
He's the one that takes your loot.

He's a calmer charmer, lady harmer,
Bullshit farmer & in your pyjamas:
Watch out for his changing mode.
There's no palaver, no stigmata,
He's a husband, he's a father
A lothario: if you'd rather.

The man works out and he's a player;
Can you resist? You haven't a prayer.
His occupation: "woman layer",
His best asset: "being a stayer".

Watch out ladies here he comes,
Not firing blanks from his big gun.
You're in love but he's in fun,
Chameleon man – run, run, run.
Watch out ladies, it's no joke,
He's just looking for someone to poke,
He seems such a decent caring bloke,
Chameleon man in his coloured cloak.

2009

## Lovers In Bed After Sex

FEMALE:
She said, "You are my friend; I'll love you to the end
When you die I will be brave, I will be there at your grave
I'll weep and not pretend and every Sunday I will spend
Putting flowers on your shrine, though dead you are still mine.
And when my ashes blow, I will reunite our souls
You were made to be my mate; we were bound by common fate".

MALE:
"Of course we are", he said, laid there on the bed
Wondering about her bra size, stroking her inner thighs
Musing on her mushy state, dreaming about her bessie mate
Then he did plausibly confide, "I'll forever be by your side".

2008

## Sales Meeting

I don't want to go in, Express by Holiday Inn.
Analysis is where we begin, talking Sales that we can win.
And what we need to underpin: I take this bullshit on the chin.

A bloke from Scotland tells a tale, an anecdote of how he made a sale,
Trying to get a laugh to no avail, stupid grey-haired bearded male,
Full of buzzwords like the gate to great trail; vapidity & rhetoric prevail.

Customer Intimacy, Customer Stroking, Customer Focussed: Thought Provoking,
I think to myself are they joking? Laugh out loud then pretend I'm choking,
Avoiding it seeming like I am fun poking, that there's a secret I am cloaking.

Faceless people holding shares, some on boards and some the Chairs,
Offshore accounts, to buy their wares and for me they have no cares,
Sales meeting up the stairs, pompous pawns with arrogant airs.

Pigs talking about their feed, I have a life, but I don't have greed,
I have no pretence, I have no need, in making our toiling workers bleed.
I play along but I'm not your breed, an end to this is what I need.

The biscuits, buffet, coffees & teas, served by the PA who's called Denise,
There is global modern business disease, all those here are but little fleas,
"ARSEHOLES" whoops! (I sneeze!) Sales meeting – NO MORE PLEASE!

2008

## If The World Ends Tomorrow

The world may stop for you, you may exit,
And you wouldn't even have time to text it,
And your friends wouldn't have time to read it
If the world ends tomorrow, they wouldn't need it.
We don't look crazy, and the world is not mad.
The pop songs are still playing & my young lad
Isn't bothered about apocalypse as he plays on Halo 3
Unaware of catastrophe, just aware of his Wii,
Which I queued for in Argos in 2007
From half past 8 until quarter to eleven.
And now it's over, in the big scale of things
It means absolutely zilch as the fat lady sings.

Your guns, bombs, power and pretence
Mean zero when there clearly is no defence
To the forces of nature to rip you asunder,
Forces of nature at which you'd marvel and wonder.
But no one will view these forces in awe
And logic gets me to ask: what was it for?
Like a joke with no punch line, poem without rhyme,
Like a clock without batteries never telling the time,
Like a ten-bob call girl without pimps or madams,
Life had no point and meant sweet Fanny Adams.

The world ends tomorrow for all that you know!
Stop for a minute and reflect before you go.
Would a universe exist without intelligence in it?
Can God simply destroy it, and did he begin it?
It's a troublesome proposition, my logic betraying
Tomorrow might end so will you be praying?

17th March 2009 (at M62 Birch Services West)

# My Devil On The Road To Wigan Pier

The devil came up to Wigan, he was searching for a soul,
I was working there on business; I was looking where to go.
So, I stopped to ask the devil (who was out my soul to steal)
He said, "Hey dude, it's the devil", I said, "Hi, my name is Neil".

"I understand you're lost," he said, with overt double entendre,
"You have so little time left to wastefully spoil and squander.
My proposition is simple, your life happy from now to lead
I can grant you that my friend, and a promise you will succeed.
It's all yours for a lifetime, joy, happiness and wealth,
Money, promotion, fame, and looks and a nice clean bill of health."

"What do you want from me Old Nick?" I say all kind of wary.
"Easiest peasiest of wants young Neil, nothing dark or scary.
"I am the devil, I know, and that makes for a bad press.
In fact, I am a real decent beast well...sort of, more or less.
So, let me tell you how it is, straight to bottom line.
I've been watching you with the women & I have seen your crime.

I've seen how emotionally & cruelly, you used all those girls,
Then persecuted yourself so bad & hid in your own world.
You need not be so mixed up, if at the end I can keep your soul.
I'll take away your guilt from you if you will just enrol.
Straight up, act now my son & you can be a winner
You'll struggle for heaven anyway being such a sinner.
So, what say you?" he says, all full of zest & (evil) spirit.
"Face it, your life is void, so now is your chance to fill it!"

The devil came up to Wigan, he was looking for a soul,
I was working there on business; I was looking where to go.
The devil offered to help me & though I didn't reply,
I thought about the life I lead & what happens when I die.
I blanked the hungry devil, waved farewell with mortal hand,
Doing what I do best, burying my head in the sand.
If you can't face up to your demons, there can be no cheer,
I realised this small fact my friend on the Road to Wigan Pier.

10th March 2009

# I Like Your Van

I like your van, the woman said to the man.
She thought him a dogger in a red Astramax van.
"Well, they just call 'em Astra's now," he said, mildly offended,
"And they were not made in this red," he said, as his prick extended.
"I have a comfy blanket, so you have no need to get dirty."
"I don't mind being dirty," she said, all menacing and flirty.
"But I don't want dust on your stockings and plaster in your hair."
She pointed to her face and said, "No, plaster me there!"

The van was a rocking, the rabbits were a clockin',
Cum juices were oozing, gay men out cruisin',
The night was bitter but deep in the shitter,
She was warm and receptive, loosely deceptive.
As he whispered in her ear, "It's got disc brakes on the rear".
"Well keep off the brakes and fuck me for fuck sakes."

In the nearest farmhouse, adorned with green shutters,
That are shut up tight, on this cold winter's night.
Is Marge. She is pretty fat, not quite Mariette,
From The Darling Buds of May? who Zeta-Jones played?
But horny nonetheless in her purple hippie dress.
Frank the Farmer, sexually calmer to the point of duress
Avoids Marge the merrymaker and like Fru T Bunn Baker
Spins his wife a yarn about the amount of time spent in barn,
Minimises time spent in house to avoid his promiscuous spouse.

Is there some elixir in the water? Seems every single daughter
Grows hornier than her mother, as one generation succeeds another.
And kinkier they become, starting with a teasy twerking bum,
From a simple grope and snogging to watersports and flogging.
The males haven't sussed it out and what this is all about.
Where males once rampantly cavorted, now their virility's is being thwarted.
A dominant gender is arising, and it should not be so surprising,
Evolution of the masses is now favouring the lasses.
Men were rubbish to the core, brought famine, conflict and war.

"I like your van," she said, "a good place for a quick screw."
Men used women for so long but now who is using who?

2008

## A Photograph from Cromer from 2006

Why do we get old? The pictures freeze the time
Queueing up to die, headstones lay in line
Like the procession of life accelerating
Towards an uncertain end,
For you, for me and the baby there
For all your family and your friends.

On a sunny day a picture, my shadow in the sun
On a putting green in Cromer, beside my infant son
He is eighteen now stands 6 foot tall, a greater man than me
I'm shown putting a white golf ball
And wonder "what became of me?"

People have to age,
Go lame then pass away,
For what is the point in that?
Life goes on or so they say.

Is there a master plan?
Will I reincarnate?
Or will I be like Peter Pan?
Perhaps I will levitate
Up to heaven or drop to hell?
Come death or Armageddon
At the time of Reaper's bell
Will I float or merely deaden
In loneliness and ownliness
Never to realise holiness or soulful bliss
Have homelessness in the dark abyss?

Could I be a ghost to spook someone?
Will my old dog be waiting yon?
Who will remember us when we're gone?
Sigh... A picture to reflect upon.

12th October 2015

**Poem Intro**

While working on business in the town of Aschaffenburg (Germany) my interpreter and fellow businessman, Sven took me to a restaurant where I saw a brown-haired lady and our eyes locked in a moment in time. I thought about who she was, her story and whether this was a look of romantic intrigue.

# 2 Seconds in Aschaffenburg

In a meagre bedsit in Aschaffenburg, a Duisburg woman resides;
She escaped her man Egbert Rottenburger (in whose manner is implied).
She is 48 years, feels grey though her hair is still naturally brown.
She dreams of a man to sweep her from this stagnant bar in town.
She walked Amflosshafen adjacent the Main lit by silver light,
Passing an autumnal Schloss Johannisburg on this drizzly night.

In this tranquil town on Bavaria's cusp, she gazed at the building adjacent
Her mind a trouble blunderbuss, for her life seemed bargain basement.
In the restaurant later our eyes met, oh magic woman of mystery
We smile, rejoice then privately grieve in a flash 2 seconds in history.
Yet in this microcosm of time, a moment of knowing, we had something special together.
The irony is a crime, love's quark of time we wanted to last forever.

Oct 2008

# Haunted

I am here and you are there
I stare at you
I want you to
Forgive me
Though I'm Dead, I'm not forgot.
I plead with you
And need you to
Acquit Me.

I did bad deeds and broke your heart
Died unforeseen
Just in my teens
I'm broken.
A better man if I had known
The joy of souls
The Dead Sea Scrolls
Unspoken.

I'm dead but live in tortured limbo
Seeing your face
A lost embrace
Please Hold Me.
But I cannot hold, and you cannot see
And somehow
I'm Haunted now
Forgive me.

06th September 2017

## Reason To Get Drunk At Your Own Wedding

The arrow of time marches like an army of ghosts
Walking on to the music of the solemn "Last Post".
Second by second, and each second is decay,
40,000 cells from the body, are lost each and every day.

All your loved ones, pain, joy and woe
Fizzle out from memory the longer time will go.
All your love and art, all your laughter and tears,
Every moment of your life will be forgot in years.

The pain and joy, the love and the hate,
What was it for when there is no fate?
Even the comets and stars, the sun and the moon
Will decay to nothing in a cauldron of doom.
Nil can have existed when nothingness exists,
So, on that thought now, I am going to get pissed.
So, if tonight won't be a memory when we are all dead,
Just drink and be merry on the day that we're wed.

2016

# Just Fuck It

When the world is lost
And no one cares
And no fingers crossed
Can't afford repairs
And a black cloud sits
Over your head
And you admit
You are better off dead.
When you are being played
Like a little puppet
Forget that you prayed
And just think "Fuck It".

Maybe you are broke
All hope seems gone
No helping folk
You are just one
Unattainable what is in your bucket
Oh well that's life so just say "Fuck It".

2007

## Elvis Man

Elvis Man, he's 45
In a dinner suit
On a special night
Not going back
To the old times
A trip in the past
Pissed to the last
Every night on the town
Kebabs and drugs
Tarts and thugs
So let's rock 'n' roll
Cheer up this hole
It's Memphis no?
Elvis Man, he's 45.

It's a bleak scene
Now back in jeans
Locked in as Fonz
Oh, Elvis Man
He's down the pan
But never moans
Prozac and comb
2-item socket
His 2 back pockets
Being cool ain't cool
Being a lad ain't bad
Sad that he is sad
Sad that he is dad.

On the wretched scene
The old ways have seen
Life takes its toll
Rock 'n' roll
Elvis Man, what's the plan?
Rock 'n' roll.

2009

**Poem Intro**

At 59, I still played football but clearly felt it was a struggle. This relates to the title of a Shakira song and my predicament at the time.

# Hips Don't Lie

I'm aching from football, when oh when will I retire?
Something makes me go back and needlessly perspire
And withstand those aching ankles, and drain me of any zest
Week after week committed, I go through the same test.
It's alright moaning in poems, and relating through minor wit
But "Hips Don't Lie" says Shakira, so maybe time to quit.

Now each day passing is so precious, one day it will be gone;
The pleasure of the present is spoiled by this phenomenon.
Every day is a miracle and I try not to be so morbidly drastic,
In believing that the aging process renders me a spastic.

If I went back 30 years, what different would I do?
Lead a healthier lifestyle? Go places I wanted to?
My knees are creaky memorials to a youth that I once knew,
"Hips Don't Lie", Shakira, oh how very true!

2017

# Art Critic

Art deco, art nouveau, modern art from heart,
Art critic, art cynic, all dandy and beau
With your eloquence bringing interpretation,
Fluffy and clever, like it's divination
In relation to what this art might show.

Art critic, art cynic, and expert in field,
Art attacks, art packs, monochrome & dayglow
With convoluted banter, bringing meaning
Which isn't there, fair and square
Over my head or maybe I'm slow
Picking up, fathoming out, what it's about.
Art man, art expert, well genned-up
On intellectual bullshit ex-Winchester or Eton
Your rationale's got me beaten.
But think on expert; ex is a has-been
And a spurt is a drip under pressure!
Maybe that's just about your measure.
Art critic, art cynic reviewing the next national treasure
It wears thin, your egoistic spin,
You want to impress with words on the backs of others
Art critic, art lovers? Put your reviews in the bin.

18/09/21

## Swingers Anon

A bloke at work said that I should go on
Something called Swingers Anon.
So, I went online and looked upon
Naked profiles by the tonne,
From Bristol to Brum & to West Brom.
Bodies in G-strings & tiny thongs
For sex at home, dogging or in the john.
There's fannies and trannies & a pensioner called Ron,
So, if there's a face you aspire to sit on
It's yours for grabs at Swingers Anon,
Well… Swingersanon.com.

I don't recommend it: don't get me wrong,
Religious people may well frown upon
And avoid it please if you feel so strong
Just make sure your content filter is on.
I make no judgement, my views aren't strong,
They do their own thing, sing their own song.
Suppose you gotta live a little before you're gone.
What is your view and thoughts upon
Joining me on Swingersanon.com?

When the wife is at work you can go on
And look up a playmate while she is gone.
Discretion assured so no harm done,
It's harmless, charmless bawdy fun,
Better than solo sex when you are one.
No dating or waiting, instant sex.com.
Same day meet, greet and jump upon,
Could be a neighbour or anyone.
There's wives, mothers, mothers' lovers and sons,
Variety is spice when all is said and done.
Fake tits, botox lips, dicks small & long,
Take your pick & dip your wick
At Swingersanon.com.

There are profile names like cuckoldjohn,
SSBBWSue & dom4fun,
Big bazookas, gym-toned buns,
Nudists bathing in the sun.
Timewasters, pic collectors you should shun
420, druggies, drunks & low life scum.
There's grandmas who prefer it up the bum
And one-line messages such as "Hiya Hun"
Folk who can't spell, some plain old dumb
Life is rich at Swingersanon.com

If you think swinging's a rare phenomenon,
Every 12 homes will have at least one.
So next time you are driving down the M1,
Wonder how many drivers are on Swingersanon.com!

22nd April 2022

**Poem Intro**

Me & my wife Claire were going to a local poem evening one night and the same day I asked her when her sister Andrea (whose partner is Robert) was coming over. She has a reputation for answering a simple question with a long answer often going way off the subject of the question and her sense of geography is somewhat confused. This is an example of that trait she has.

# Simple Question

Ask I, "What time is Andrea coming Claire?"
Reply she, "Well she went out yesterday somewhere
Not sure where, think it began with L
Was it Lagos or Leyton or Whatstandwell?
Anyway, she says Robert can repair that eave
There's a ladder in our garage I do believe
Sez, they have a ladder but no way to bring it
I've a poem for tonight; should I sing it?"
"No", I say, "It's not an open mic."
"Oh - a four-page poem has Carlton Mike
And Elaine's got three, so I believe
And I think Ruth has a few up her sleeve
Only YOUR poems that swear like troopers
Andrea is looking to get a Mini Cooper."
I cut her off with impatient stare:
Ask I, "What time is Andrea coming Claire?"

01st May 2022

# Shop Window Shock

It took an age to get here,
It seems like a very long time,
It's only a period of years,
To bring about this design.
The brain still feels no sign of age,
It still likes music and sport,
But the body it acts as my cage
So, watching is the last resort.
Whether it be rugby or footy
OK, I can still play bowls,
But 'fraid my legs turn to putty
Just my thinking about sporting roles.
So, more time spent in my armchair
Thinking of glories long since gone,
I put my glasses down but where?
I can't see nowt without them on.

This age was always coming
Since I was just a pup
So why am I humming
Waites' "I Don't Want to Grow Up"?
And why am I whistling & singing
Past a shop window that I clock,
Thinking my clothes were slimming
The image back is a shock.
Heavyset is a word to describe me
A fat fucker perhaps be more apt
Stiff walking on my worn knees
Getting old is definitely crap.

25th August 2022

**Poem Intro**

I visited Ulley Parish Church on my own one day and found it peaceful and a great place to reflect. I sat there all alone in the church considering all the self-induced turmoil I had suffered and caused to others in my relationships. I turned around and had this sort of prophetic vision where I saw a girlfriend I hardly knew, walking in all dressed in a white wedding gown looking radiant and beautiful. I was dead against marriage at that point but the vision inspired me to write this poem and it is called "Universe's Blessing" as I felt that a great power was maybe communicating with me. I did end up marrying her some years later though not at this beautiful church alas as it proved a little over our budget. This is about the vision, not real events.

# The Universe's Blessing

Let not my glories pass away,
"Abide With Me", I sing and say.
My love is with me on this day,
Let not this love e'er pass away.
Like those we hear who died before
For many, life was just a chore.
Some died empty, meek and poor,
Some died without love at their core
A lonely life for to endure.

The Lord my Shepherd from a place above
Ordains me with this special love,
One so apt it fits like a glove.
Showing me a sign: a glass-stained dove
That soars in front with static grace
Two souls, two hearts attuned embrace
In this my very special place.
I discovered when I first saw her face
This special place that made me so in awe
Was matched by her beauty and sweet allure.
A vision of a love so pure
Is sanctified by this place for sure.

We prayed with the flock in Lord God's House
To love our neighbours, avoid bad rows.
But today we really made our vows
With me as hers and her my spouse.
I could read her body, from feet to head
I had a map of her like an A to Z.
She vowed to be with me and be wed
"I love you Neil" is what she said.
My heart is hers and hers eternal
I made my vows in mind internal
To feature soon in a Parish Journal

As Mr & Mrs Richardson Taylor Bliss
My Dear Claire Marie as my Missus.

30/10/11

**Poem Intro**

This is a whimsical look at Withernsea, not a critique. It really is more about how our seaside resorts withered and became run down following the railway closures of the '60s Beeching era and the reach of ordinary people now able to holiday in the Mediterranean where the weather is more consistent.

## Withernsea

This town is somewhere you might go maybe,
Got to say it's not everyone's cup of tea.
It's a Holderness Town not too far from me;
Kay Kendall was a famous escapee.
It's a town that sits on the A1033
With the prime meridian just out at sea.
With pier towers but no pier to see
And no harbour or a quay
And you'll struggle to find a herbal tea
Though there's cafes... well at least three.
And a kids' play area that's there for free
With a spongy surface to keep falls pain free.
A lighthouse it has; but where it be?

In the middle of town not near the sea,
It was built circa 1893.
I suppose boats can see it to a degree
It's high and the view is there to see,
7 feet lower than the highest tree
In the UK, and it has a cheap entrance fee
And all the under 5s can get in free.
Poets rave about places you should be
And though I'm far from the bourgeoisie
I'm no snob, I like to come here me,
Choose this place and go sightsee.
If you like Maltby and like the sea
Go to the East Riding; Withernsea.

19th May 2022

## Recluse

The bubbles were rising in my lager
Outside a pub, seeking Nirvana
But a builder's bum in the panorama
And smells of fags and marijuana
Made me yearn my striped pyjamas.

I love the spring, love this time of year,
I love country pubs & a pint of beer,
Love babbling brooks & a foamy weir
But even this beauty they do besmear
There's people everywhere to ruin it here.

As soon as I step out of my front door
I start being judged by society's law
Am I bi, gay, fat or poor?
They're judging me & that's for sure.
I shouldn't care, wish I could ignore
But like you, these thoughts are to the fore
In this civil status social war,
Lord make me disappear into the floor.
For there is anxiety and stress times more galore
I'm going home, can't take much more.

I've come out and am just about
To journey out to Kinder Scout
Well, more the country round about
I have walked 200 yards and hear a shout:
"This is private land now please get out!"
Voiced by a well-to-do, who's posh and stout
A landed gentry who has local clout,
Looked like a Michael Winner cardboard cut-out.

I turned tail and headed for
The path that leads up to Mam Tor
Hoping that my faith would restore
By virtue of fab views on this detour.
But sure as eggs and sure as sure
This deviation was no quick cure
For a chatty lady who is 64
Wanted to walk with me upon the moor
And so spare me from this frightful bore.
When she had gone I said "no more"
And made haste to the sanctuary of my front door.

Even going out for just a drive and cruise
Exposes me to idiots on the loose.
Some have indicators that they never use
I try and stay calm, not blow my fuse.
Some have not got the faintest clues
My scorn and frustration starts to ooze
Gives me the "going out blues".
So maybe baby I will choose
My temper and happiness not to lose,
Not subject myself to this abuse.
Come join me get in my shoes
And become a hermit or a recluse.

March 2022

# Dog Dirt

I'm a lawful guy, not dodgy or shifty,
I'm not a miser, though a little thrifty.
I like to travel, like to be nifty
But sod me all the "A" Roads are fifty.

I like pedal to the metal, though I'm no nutter,
I like to carve through the land like a knife through butter.
But so many yellow cameras with a hungry shutter
And police speed vans slyly parked in the gutter.

I don't wish to sound like a grumpy old man
But I can go faster on a dirt track in Iran.
You know real crime solving is an "also ran!"
When there's money to be made from a mobile van.

And talking of mad men: there's loads on the street
Lonely, dirty, no home or retreat,
No funds for services, no cops on the beat,
No social care. And is this how we treat
Social inequality, anxiety, mental health,
An empire of "common" but with no wealth.

This griping is old, this moaning well worn,
The elite of the world have faithfully sworn
To get rich and richer and have us all torn
And have us all focus on Netflix and Porn.
But nothing changes when it comes to hunger and scorn,
My poem is pointless as there's no one to warn.
Who takes any notice? So it's all forlorn
There's no dog shit chucked on a rich mans lawn.

2003

# The Anti-Capitalist Rant

Retail therapy, the crave won't stop
Online, Amazon, down at the shops
Yet skint, skinned, thrifty not,
More clueless than the Keystone Cops.
When it comes to the money crop,
Try it, buy it, fly to the top,
Food, clothes, gear and pop,
A red letter through the box will drop,
Retail therapy: the crave won't stop.

Go to Meadowhall or Junction 32,
Stuck in traffic, stuck in a queue,
With likeminded suckers just like you
Dying for a frappe or a brew.
Cost at Costa is £12.92
Then a ton for Timberland shoes
Def not gold but sold as new.
Sold a pup - start barking you!
You are sagging & gagging, need a cappa,
Resistance & resolve is getting crapper,
You'd buy owt if it were in a wrapper,
Culture says buy so does a rapper,
Called Archie, who says Versace
Makes you a man and Saatchi & Saatchi
Say avoid pink, lilac and khaki.

A chilled smarty at a dinner party
Raves on 'bout being cool and arty
And how keeping up with fashion partly
Bestows class and a makes a lass
Look the part and not tarty.
Black belt in fashion not karate
What a way to go, reap what you sow
So, send out for the searching party
To happiness you used to know.

Goods made: recycled, new or fresh,
Made in Taiwan or Bangladesh,
Imported cheap for a shopping sesh.
Love thy neighbour, vote cheap labour,
Sweat and blood wore on your flesh
Crazed shoppers from Ely to Inverness.

Your stereotypical car is in the city
Where the Warboys committee made signs pretty.
Gap insurance bought, good you thought.
Things you don't need and it's profoundly shitty,
I'm trying to make a point not just write a ditty.
So please be taught if happiness be sought
Focus less on the stuff that you have bought.

I don't want to take your very precious time
By reciting this rant that comes as rhyme.
You may consider that your life is fine
By comparing goods: yours versus mine.
I just wish not to condone a moral crime
And approve a society in corrupt decline.
So be your happiest and not a capitalist
And love and truth be thine.

June 2022

# Failure On Normans Bank, Peak District

To railway work I was deeply wed,
I only wish I could have stayed in bed.
With an ominous dark foreboding dread
I signed on at the loco shed.
'Twas cold and wet and the Beaufort scale
Was telling of speeds that it deemed gale.

Oh, what joy to drive a train
In darkest Peak, at night, in rain.
The heaviest load for loco strain
Over snotty rails on goods and main,
Past semaphores, through sections long
Yet sensing something was quite wrong.
Through Cowburn Tunnel, 2 miles long,
The engine climbed and did not feel strong,
Doing only 10 though a modest climb,
Slipping, sanding, losing time.
The joints passed slow and clinked in rhyme,
Heckling me for a fictitious crime
Of just being there upon that line
And being unnerved by this incline.
Bad portents and important signs
Like screeching wheels and exhaust whine
Were telling me that all was not fine.

Out of tunnel then downhill with speed,
Shut the throttle for there's no need,
Coasting is the way to drive
Descending the 1 in 75
Past Edale's 'home signal' burning green
And past Mam Tor that can't be seen
Hiding behind the rain and cloud...
Then suddenly a light comes proud,
Lighting my cab with vermillion glow,
A fault light that translates as a no-go.
The engine stops, the brakes apply,
From loco break blocks sparks do fly,
I hope it's something that I can sort
And recall a fault that I was taught.
With ship to shore now on the blink,
Gosh I need to really think
Is it a fuse or a CCB?
Or is it providence stopping me?
Whatever I try it's plain to see
I have no answer, am all at sea.

Time quickly passes and all around
Wind and rain are the only sound
But I have to walk; I may be drowned.
With dark and black as my surround,
With bending boughs and whistling gale
And telegraph wires like shipping rope sails,
Rain in my eyes like a scorpion's tail
I walk the track trying to prevail
To find a lineside phone to no avail.

Whipping winds with cracking branches,
Thunderous roars like avalanches,
Cacophonies like screaming banshees
That wail at me in squalls and tranches,
Which overwhelm my varied senses
All trapped in by railway fences,
Imagining irrevocable consequences
Exposed without any defences.

A landslide perhaps, falling scree
From Normans Bank right next to me
And a yelling, swelling River Noe
Roars underneath the bridge below
Whose rusty, wet fence tears my hand,
So that blood trickles upon command
To the forces of nature sent so cruel
Manifest themselves as though a ghoul.
This is murder, it is no duel,
The puddle has become a pool.
I am a frightened, battling wounded soldier
Who then slips from the ballast shoulder
Into mud, and a pool no less
That fills the baiting hungry cess
Far from any road access:
I then pass out from my distress.

A light I then see in my eyes
For to me it would be no surprise.
I know what happens when one dies
When the soul departs the body & flies
To the bright light up in the skies.

"You OK?" transcendentally spoken,
Is this heaven where I'm awoken?
But wait, I still feel cold and feel pain,
I feel wet and still feel rain,
I feel a throbbing in my head
And this recline no feather bed.
"You OK mate?" once again said
And then I know I am not dead.

The kind farmer had come to my aid
And helped me up from where I laid.
His 4x4 took me through a glade
Through a copse all bowing and swayed
Past nooks of land and weathered rocks
To Earles Sidings Signal Box.

I recount to thee this tale of woe,
That haunts me now where e'er I go.
And from then unto the present day
I drove no more on iron way.

2022

**Poem Intro**

True tale just setting off from Southampton up the Channel on a Norwegian Fjords cruise with my wife.

## My First Cruise (And With Someone I Love)

"Anything from the bar?"
"No ta...
It's a bit dear"
"You're on your hols..?"
"OK then, a beer...
But no cocktail"
As we set sail
Down the Solent
Out past Wight

In dimming light
Past Cowes ferry
Looking very
Twinkly at sea
And you and me
Hold hands and we
Cuddle. Not surprising
Looking at the horizon
In happy entwine
Gorgeously mine
And her love shines.
An illuminated coastline
Reflects in the brine
Us… happily wed
Has to be said
Cruising through life
With a perfect wife
The only one I'd choose
We are on a love cruise.

10th September 2022

## What My Dad Said

My dad said to me that ten years after being christened
He got parental advice, but that he never listened
To his dad: so he merely learned life's lessons alone.
His dad's advice he never heeded and so he pleaded
With me to listen to him, to every sentence, word and letter
And not be like him, but to heed and do much better.

Even though, he knew, I would not listen, as I grew
I could never be like him, or even my sister Lynn
Or Paul my elder bro, who I know, was sporty and thin
Just like his dad, who is my dad and of our kin
Each have their own skin: different but related.
My Dad found out, albeit rather belated,
His dad's advice may well have translated
Into an easier life for him, if only he had noted
And followed the words that his dad had quoted.

You know, when all is said, and all is done
We all have troubles by the tonne.
My mum, worried for her son (me)
Nay more, she worried for kids all three.
Worry is bad, but being a dad, I understand
We want to be there to hold their hand,
We want it to turn out just like we planned,
And control their lives on our command.

My dad said, from his wise head
You will do better and be a go-getter
If my advice, you follow right.
But kids will never see the light
And that's OK, it is just the way
Nature is and so I say
Please make this vow
To follow the principle of Tao.
Life is a stream, so do not be hollow,
It is the stream that you should follow.
Your dad's advice is meant well to do
But he is he and you are you.
"My dad said" and I pondered on
Some things I did right and others wrong
"My dad said" things I'll rue to my grave,
Still I thank my dad for the words he gave.

2022

**Poem Intro**

Not in the best of taste but my wife's father was out in Spain where he was on family business with his wife when he became terminally ill. He had a fall prior to his journey there. All of what is in the poem is based on true events.

## Is Your Dad Dead Yet?

He went t' Spain, knew he shun't
Shoulda told ya mum, shoulda been blunt.
He was weak, he weren't that well;
Remember his bungalow when he fell?
Now will he last? Wouldn't like t' bet
Hey up Claire, is your Dad dead yet?

In hospital it is touch and go,
He had a stroke and a further blow.
Bladder screwed, pneumonia and ill,
He was s'posed to die but he's got a strong will.
He gets better, worse then stet
I say Claire, Is your Dad dead yet?

They brought him home ready to die;
We were told he'd passed but it was a lie.
We told everyone that he was deceased,
Condolences had been received
But status is still "non dead", so do not fret
And let's ask Claire if her Dad's dead yet.,

Bless him for the big man don't wanna go
Despite his funeral booked two weeks ago.
Not sure whether he's had his last rites
It's costing your mum a packet in flights!
She'll be dying 1st or else end up in debt
Now then Claire, is your Dad dead yet?

It's aged us all and that's for sure
He defies death despite no cure,
Ice cream no but morphine yes,
Your mum is under extreme duress.
"Dad you can pass" you said he could.
Telling him he could die you thought was good.
No wonder the poor bloke's bed is wet,
Hey up Claire is your Dad dead yet?

28/03/23

**Poem Intro**

This poem references Edith Wharton's tragic book, Ethan Frome, hence the title, Mr E Than. It is about being trapped by your materialistic home comforts. The parody is about being stuck to a life where you cannot break free because of circumstances. In Wharton's book this was about a sense of duty to an invalid wife but with a desire for his wife's cousin. In this case Mr E Than cannot break free because of his materialistic gizmos and lifestyle.

# Mr E Than

Soulless handsome man with a tan
Waits in for the Amazon van
With shoulders like boulders.
A parcel-carrying man
Brings next-day stuff to Mr E Than.

Than has Netflix and a firestick pressed
Into a USB port. He's a VIP guest
To film and TV; he's alive, not free.
Choosing a life that is second best
Not enhancing the gift with which he's blessed.

I could write Than a biographical book
And point out where he came unstuck.
He's stuck at home, like Ethan Frome.
Joy is stuck, like Zeena's luck.
Worries of his own, like a garden gnome
Looking up in awe at Becher's Brook
Like a timid, limp clueless cuck
Choosing to lose and let life suck.

2022

**Poem Intro**

A few of us oldies get together on a Monday morning for a natter to put the world to rights and just chat about anything. Religion, war, politics, history, music, geography, cost of living etc are all prime topics. This poem is just based on the over exaggerated characters who attend and it is not factual, just exaggerated.

# Thoughts at Men's Morning

I have nothing to offer you Jesus;
I will sit at your table bare.
I got my soul and my spirit
And nothing to fill it
Can I come and see you up there?

Now I'm a right one to ask you
And a naïve artist poetry-wise.
But down here in Blighty
My Mum's nearly ninety
Will you take her upstairs when she dies?

Got a guy here with me called Harry:
He's a Christian through and through.
He scoffs at Allah
Don't believe in Valhalla
His life is a joy coz of you!

Our mate Ron hails from a village called Whitwell:
Can see lots of things in the world that are bad.
He wears a beret as cap,
A unique clever sort of chap,
And his fastidious faith is no fad.

Ron's wife and himself had differences
Which I'm now told are reconciled.
He believes in the Letters of Paul
But has built up this wall
Where the 'Good Book' acts as his guide.

Whereas Roger is a stout non-believer,
Yet he once taught the Alpha Course.
But there is a twist
For now he's a Humanist
That's an atheist with Christian cause.

He scoffs at The Church of England,
At Catholics, Muslims & Jews.
He reckons he got wise
To all the nonsense & lies
And that religion has political use.

Another Harold makes a guest appearance;
He assumes he is the Lord's fountain head.
He advises others on the bible
With no risk of libel
Understands every word Jesus said.

*View From Here*

Now Jesus it is me here who is speaking,
Thinking I'm sort of middle of the road & quite wise.
Psychologically strong
And know right from wrong
Viewing them with unbiased eyes.

Because I've looked at it from every angle,
Not a scientologist me like Tom Cruise.
I'm not a romancer
And I don't know the answer
But you sure ain't leaving no clues.

Maybe when I am wizened and failing,
My breath short and eyesight all blurred,
I might cling to a faith
And view death as safe
Based on your biblical illogical word.

Until that day comes my sweet Jesus,
I will see you as a human who came
With no false pretence
To speak for spiritual sense
And extol love and never feel shame.

Men's morning it gets you thinking,
Debating religion & how things once were.
Other's views valid they be
They are different to me
And I guess that is why I am there.

Feb 2023

## Love Thy Neighbour

Worried and skint, guess we need to get a grip
On Personal Independence otherwise known as PIP.
Brain is on fire, mental health is dire,
Too old to work, too young to retire.
Summer rains pour, the roads are wet,
Haven't got it quite figured out just yet.
One hand in pocket, two pockets of nowt
"Britain on Benefits": you've heard the quote.
We got a watch, we got a phone,
So why have we the right to moan,
Says pensioner Gwen from Erith, Kent
Who's mentally crippled and she is hell bent
On seeing asylum seekers refused access here.
She is wrath personified yet full of fear
And an ardent member of a neighbourhood watch
Who voted Brexit to stop immigrants flock
Into her world of sheer shell shock control.
She's a fear-riddled, worried, busy-bodied little soul
Who says all should work, if not no dole,
No unions either, no miners or coal.
And hard labour for slackers: "arbeit macht frei",
She's a neo-Nazi hippy who always lets fly
With her views and opinions like countless more
There's no arguing with those with a settle to score!

There are a million minions down and out
And millions more are lost.
There are millions more in this cruel world
Who follow blindly at their cost.

Find fear in the counties, or the Parish of St. Giles
Where elegies and cemeteries blend in the country miles.
From Stoke Poges to Stokesley, Stoke-on-Trent or Crewe,
Acknowledge the suffering sufferers get, who are fighting just like you.
So, chav or toff, sneeze or cough, we all need to see the light.
Let's take our foot off the gas then it might be alright.
Choose not to scorn but accept and love your imperfect fellow man.
It's hard to do. Tell me about it! But happen yes it can.

10th May 2023

## In Limoux

In Limoux, sipping coffee and cider
Sat in bar, with me beside her.
Café society, Vive la France
Could I live here? Just give us a chance!
In Limoux on the banks of the Aude
She likes it here and je suis d'accorde.

St Martin's cathedral, republic square
In Brasserie Le Commerce, sat in chair,
5 Years hence, you and me and kisses,
Occitania: Do you fancy it Mrs?

15th March 2023

# Pine

One day I will be in a box of pine
But let me say until that time
I am yours and you are mine
Rightly matched by our star signs.
Even after death be thine
Through the thick and thin and grime
Of life, and though our ages climb
Me with coffee and you with wine
Happily "marriedly" we entwine.
You are true beauty & divine
That I worship like a shrine.
I need no money to be fine
With you I have my own gold mine.
One day I will be in a box of pine
Which is apt, for it is you I pine.

13th February 2023

## Calvary or Carvery

Oh Lord, this place ain't Calvary
But I have a cross to bear
Sat in a pub in a carvery
On a Mayfair dining chair.
There's two for the price of one
Served between two and four
But the steak pie is sold out
And pallid chips are raw.

Wetherspoon's or Stonehouse,
Sizzler or the Flaming Grill,
My Mum gets ketchup down her blouse
And says she can feel a chill.
She dates back to the mid-thirties,
Memory is nowhere near what it once was,
I wash her towels and her dirties
In the machine on a two-hour wash.
She goes out on a limited basis,
No more than a 4-mile range,
My dad parks in disabled places
And is always dropping his change.
He's got nose hairs that predate UNESCO
But he can still do well in a quiz,
They're both season ticket holders at Tesco's
In the café there that is.

You can't bring trollies in the café,
It's against all the fire regs.
They order two lattes piping hot
And insist on runny eggs.

McDonald's and Greggs are other venues
As alternate places to dine,
Not brilliant in terms of menus
But pasties and chips are fine.
There are loads of places to visit
If you want to eat cheap food out.
Ok it's not all that exquisite
But it's Ok if you need to get out.
The cheap dine-out life is so good
When you can't cook, play golf or bowls,
So, when you can't walk like you once could
Cheap food works for aging souls.

June 2023

## Went To The Doctors

I went to the Doctor's Practice
And was told in no uncertain terms
"You're over the hill young man"
As he washed away my germs.

He said, "Think of it like a mountain...
Whereas once you were at your peak
Well now the slope is downwards
And it's looking rather bleak".

"You cannot walk without a hobble...
You can't convincingly run at all
You get indigestion when you gobble
And your tummy's a medicine ball."

"You need Ramipril and Amlodipine
To keep your BP to the norm
And your erection is no longer seen
When you wake up in the morn."

He says my reactions are a little tardy
And it looks like a wire brush in my nose
He says I cannot reach my knees hardly
Never mind touch my toes.

He says, "You might have been a fitty...
You once might have turned girls' heads
But now you have reached sixty
You are going to need more meds!"

"At least you get free prescriptions"
Says he in cheerful tone
"And it is candidly my prediction
You've got arthritis in your bones."

"So never mind the ageing process
Just accept the downward slope
And pray there is life that follows death
Because that will help you cope!"

June 2023

# Market Harborough

She lives in Market Harborough
By a skate park by the track,
She wanted to retire to Scarborough
But there is no turning back.
Her hubby was from Leicester,
He would not move away so far
And all his life he'd test her,
And now she bears his scar.
It's more mental than on body
Though on body he did impose,
He now thinks more about his Audi
Than those he should hold close.

The choices she made were fateful
Especially choosing him as her man,
He turned from OK to hateful
As soon as they had a pram.
He puts her down daily
Now she has no confidence at all,
Made her old and grey and pale-y
Now her soul's pinned to the wall.

In the street where she was brought up
Lives Shamia Quereshi,
Rahim her husband is caught up
In living life as a lie.
He got married to Shamia
Even though they had never met,
She is as ruthless and austere
As anyone can get.
He spends 14 hours in a taxi cab
Works 7 days on the trot,
The money is sent to the Punjab
To pay for her family's lot.
While she herself sits at home
And the kids never see their dad.
Searching for rings on Google Chrome
And phoning Faisalabad.

From Father, Sister to Mother
Freedom they mean to rob,
Or corporates or big brother
Or spouse or boss in job.
For "control" is freedom-stripping
Even done by man or wife
So don't let them catch you kipping:
Take control of your life!

August 2023

## Subconscious

What's on your mind?
What makes you tick?
Think you are bright
And def not thick?
For you laugh and smile,
You hug and hold,
You can be withdrawn,
Aloof and cold.
I understand, I really do
There are people just like you
Who want to fear
Who want to fight
Victims of fight, victims of flight.
We are beasts in non-base form,
Survival is the only norm.
It's caveman psyche without the club,
See it in your local pub.

*View From Here*

What's on your mind?
What makes you tick?
What will you choose:
Carrot or stick?
You have no say
In who you are,
You have no say in what you think,
For subconscious is the link
That overrides
And deep divides
Your best intent that you call will.
You mean well but you are still
A basic beast, the human ape
In a survival feast, you can't escape.
You are a machine, biologically driven
In a smokescreen asking to be forgiven
For sins you did, but you did not:
It was your brain that hatched the plot.
The side that which you cannot control;
The brain is parted it is not whole.
Try to improve, be morally sound,
A noble cause there to be found.
Good luck if goodness is for you sought
But I say in this report
It's hard, it is so very hard
To change your lot and swap your card
To try to change your ways, true grit you'll need
And I will pray that you succeed.

Sept 2023

**Poem Intro**

Meet my wife!

# Gadget Girl

Gadget Girl, Gimmick Gal,
She's a gimme-a-gadget PayPal pal,
Amazon, Facebook or charity shop,
Buys with her phone or on laptop,
Gadget Girl she cannot stop!

She buys small stuff, she buys big,
She has more things than thingamajig,
She has hair extensions and four wigs,
We have foldable chairs for music gigs,
I'm sure in the garage there's a whirligig,
At the side of three shovels: but we never dig!

We've got an electric soap-dispensing thing,
Fridge magnets and loads of keyrings,
We've a ball for the cat on the end of some string,
We are on our third garden swing,
Who knows what tomorrow will bring,
Pendants, charms, ornaments or bling?

We've got a tin-opener you don't need to wind,
A magnifying glass for the nearly blind,
Fake hair, fake nails, fake lashes for the face,
There is junk and clutter all over the place.

We've got dog bowls tho' we've no hound,
There're luminous toys in the garden found,
Cat bowls on stilts so it doesn't have to bend,
Numerous types of whisks with which to blend.
An electric salt and pepper shaker,
A specialist quick fire poached egg maker,
A ceramic spoon for post-plunge tea bags,
And a garage full of old corporate mags.
There are lots of tweezers to pluck her chin,
We've got a double garage you can't get in,
The parcel vans deliver from July to June,
Have to buy another house quite soon,
For this one is full there's no more room.

Gadget girl, Gimmick Gal,
I love her still and she's my pal,
Her looks would not melt the butter,
Gadget Girl and Queen of clutter.

March 2023

## Heart and the Arrow

She drew a heart with an arrow in the condensation
In her bedroom without any heat,
And though not at the point of starvation
She's just trying to make her ends meet.

Her heart was commemorating an ex called Nathan,
The brother of a crackhead next door,
He left her with his debts, from his gambling and bets,
But she still loves him despite all his flaws.

She walks down streets thronging with traffic
To collect Marnie, her daughter, from school.
Marnie is not doing that terrific, and her anxiety's prolific
And her life is troubled and cruel.

Marnie's tea is crisps and rice pudding with raisins,
A midge-modge of texture and shape
Eaten between texts, grunts and liaisons
With the TV as a means to escape.

Her mum's got a general anxiety disorder,
Poor Marnie has ADHD.
They are on Sertraline and family genes
Means that they can never be free
From dysfunctional, chaotic interactions:
There is nothing but strife, conflict and woe.
Mum drew the heart and needs a new start
But she's in love and can never let go.

The heart and arrow could still be seen reflecting
But the person who drew it not seen.
Lost love, lost hope and unable to cope,
She was taken by Benzodiazepine.

Her daughter is an orphan of a slanted system,
Maybe to follow in her mother's shoes.
There's no compassion, kindness or wisdom
And this story is no longer news.
Hence why I bring it to your attention
If you're able to stop one minute and think.
I don't know if there is a cure or prevention,
But if you care you can email a link.
Tell them you care and that it is not fair,
And that it should not be allowed to be this way.
Write nice and polite and please do not swear
And email no-one-cares@gov.uk.

Jan 2024

## The Hare and the Hound

My dog "Reg" and I were walking,
We were enjoying the evening dusk.
Walking happily through the pine trees
Through a leaf-decaying earthy musk.
In all the world; universe in fact
I had but not one single care
Until our path was rudely crossed
By a darting, brazen hare.

The dog spotted the sprinting doe ahead
And with fervour bolted hence.
He dashed into the dark, dense thicket
And leapt right over a fence.

The two thundered away in the stillness
Through the murk and now rising mist,
Until their noise subsided to silence
With vacant lead around my wrist.

I took stock of my dimming surroundings,
Noted the darkening evening light.
I shouted for him in all directions
But only mirages came to sight.
And no return I witnessed presently
Of my canine friend departed and gone.
He could be lost or trapped or shot
I had no clues to act upon.

And in which direction might I search
To boldly look for him in haste,
The direction they had thundered into?
i.e. the direction of the chase?
But how far and what deviations
And what turns did they both make?
Should I now abandon my loyal friend
And slither away like a snake?

These thoughts they froze me rigid
As the cold and chill bit home.
To numb my exposed digits
As I reached for my mobile phone.
A forest remote and dark and thick
Where no phone signal can ever be had.
A lonely, isolated forest be it
And I it's one nomad.

A rustling then I hear close by
In the brush and broom
But nothing can I nearly spy
In this rising fog and gloom.
A fox perhaps, a badger or deer
But not my dog for sure
As the deepest sense of flight and fear
Makes me tense and insecure.

My car parked yet a half a mile
From where I present stood
So, I made tracks toward it thence
Through springy grass and woods.
Yearning that he may be there
My stoic loyal friend
Be waiting for me with tail a-swish
As I reach my walking's end.

With trepid footsteps and only sound
Be the crunch beneath my feet
Up a hill to higher ground
Where path and lane they meet.
But not a lane of a busy kind
A dead end spooky, creepy lane,
Why is fate being so unkind?
As no dog there to restrain.

I shout yet again his name out loud
'Neath black lime trees overhead
With evil spirits, gremlins and ghosts
That are dancing in my head,
Imagined in this swarthy light
Amid the brambles and the trees
Where silence deafens all around
To tremble me at my knees.

A perilous choice and too numb to act
"I can't abandon him," I say
But neither can I stay here all night
I'm cursed whichever way.

When behind me flickers white light
Through fog on trees and verge
Which brightens into headlamps.
First one, then two emerge
They directly are approaching me
On the otherworldly straight behind.
I try to clock the occupants
But its lights, they keep me blind.

It stops just aft the car of mine,
I'm fearing a macabre fate.
I'm thinking of "Dual" 1971,
In a frozen fear I wait.
At last its driver appears through the fog
And seems to know I am in distress.
He asks me if I have lost a dog
I say "How did you know?" and "Yes".

He saw my wandering dog all confused
As he left his cottage up the lane
And he has my dog in his shooting brake
So, I can now see Reg again.

You cannot imagine exultation thus
To know he was safe and well.
One man and dog, well that was us
In this true story that I tell.

I offer no advice or twist,
It happened to me one night
From dread to loss to total bliss
Guess all turned out alright.

Feb 2024

## All Good Son

I was in my son's car, travelling home,
Scrolling through the news on my S9 phone.
A throwaway remark I chucked into the mix:
"World's going downhill and it's turning shit".

My son defiantly asked, "Are you real dad?
To think the world is so terrible, dire and bad?"
I say, "How do you mean, like you don't agree?"
He shook his head and said, "No, have a look-see".

He got on his high horse did the man to my right,
Said I should think more & and not talk so shite,
And not to fire from the hip, cos then nonsense flies,
And learn to think with my brain and use my eyes.
Then from his mouth bullet-pointed style,
A quick list to wipe away my smug-like smile.

"You're paid time off work, can travel where you want,
Eat world food in any type of restaurant,
Got better health, better eyes, better teeth and heart,
Better choice, better food, access to art,
With literature, music, film & TV,
Millions of evocative things to read and see.
Well, it's as good as it's been, so mark you me,
With so many places to go by air or sea,
Like holidays abroad or in the UK
There is widespread sport to watch or play.
You have little disease, famine & no plague,
And people now live to a ripe old age,
You can talk to me direct any time and place,
Prejudice is abating to all sex and race.
Can see the weather in Denver or Bangalore,
You can get products delivered next day to door,
You just moan you and you don't think what for,
When the world is amazing & you should be in awe."

"So why so shite, dad ... what do you say?"
Stupefied, I retort, "It just **IS**.... OK?"

March 2024

## Nothing to Write Home About

Had a mediocre run just late,
Nothing crap, nothing great,
Nothing to write home about,
Normal weather no flood or drought.
As a poet it's just drab and stale
Inspirational prose? Well, my words fail.
It's not melancholy, it's not bright,
It's dreary, dull, drab, and trite.
I'm not happy, I'm not glum
I may as well just suck my thumb
Than look for an inspirational crumb
So, this poem is about nowt my chum.

It's a bromidic tale weak and drab
And your attention it will not grab
And critics no need here for a confab
Forget the publishers, call a cab!
I'm going home, it's not a great prose
May as well push carpet foam up my nose,
At least then there'd be effect and cause
This poem's dedicated to saddos and bores.

Summer 2023

# Dread On the Sunbed

How do I feel? Is it just me?
As I peek from the sunbed and through my knees
To see a tanned, toned lifeguard & bikini-bronzed blonde,
Is life so hard to be a skimmer on the pond?
Full of perfect specimens and that ain't me,
It's the survival of the fittest: that's what I see.

Holidaying on beaches; it fills me full of dread,
Are they looking at me or is it all in my head?
My chest held in, my shoulders upright,
Wishing to be slender, wishing for more height.
Just wishing I didn't care and just felt alright,
But I pass reflections and it's not a pretty sight.
Paranoid about the physical, on a downer no less,
Wishing to be better, maybe even impress.
Well, that is a dream, to be cool and fit,
And not feel you look like a piece of shit.
Oh, not to care even if fat, ugly, grey or bald,
And full of moles, holes, wrinkled and old.

I'm laid on a sunbed, a sin bed in my case,
Ashamed of the sin of imperfection of place.
Ashamed how my body is, I don't want to sit up,
I want to keep laid down - hide my man-boob cup.
Laid on a sunbed, a sun worshipper I'm not,
Pains me to be exhibiting this 'ole body I've got.
These dark dungeons of flesh that shape who I am,
Shape is a pun, and I am a man
Who is far from perfect, but it'll have to do,
Is there a bit of me perhaps in all of you?

Dec 2023

# Mouse in the Garage

I was in the garage sorting out my stuff,
It was dusty and cold, and I'd had enough.
I was about to make tracks back towards the house,
When beneath a wicker chair I spied a mouse.
I looked down at the mouse and the mouse looked up,
He looked cheeky, brave and our gazes stuck.
I leaned forward but the tiny fella was not scared,
And I got as close to him as I really dared.

I felt inclined to speak to the mouse some words,
Whilst recognising by so doing was quite absurd.
"Hello Mouse," I said, "It's nice to meet."
And he replied back: "Squeak, squeak, squeak".

The mouse removed its gaze and looked away,
But in static place the mouse did stay.
I said, "I bet you are scared by this man here?"
Mouse answered not and showed no fear.

"So, mouse if you agree then just say 'squeak',
For there are many answers in life that I seek.
Is there a god or at least an afterlife?
A place not like earth all full of strife?"
But the mouse was silent, still looked away,
So, I shrugged and thought what next to say.
"Another question mouse for what it's worth,
Will the meek inherit the earth?"

The mouse, my oracle, was saying naught,
This is a silly game I shrewdly thought.
I said, "Our futures mouse appear somewhat bleak".
Piped up the mouse: "Squeak, squeak, squeak".

Feb 2024

## Revolution?

You say you want a revolution,
We all want to change the world
But tyranny is a form of evolution
Just as natural as a bee or bird.
Because we are just tailless simians,
Just nature programmed machines,
Not free-thinking empathetic civilians,
We are just wild animals in jeans.
Come the revolution should it happen
Will the capitalists have had their day?
Don't put your Che Guevara cap on just yet
Because greed will never go away.

Feb 2022

## Tick Box Land

It's a fast-food franchised outlet near
A franchised pub that sells crap beer.
Granted, its cheap but not much cheer.
Both places have toilets at the rear
And tick boxes on the walls in here.

A sure sign that they are "quality assured"
Just like in a homely hospital ward
Where Paula nurse won staff award,
Nowt to do with patients being cured.
Real service has become obscured,
She just ticked more boxes or so I heard.

In a place where zombie-like pensioners roam
There are elderly care residents being left alone
In their bedrooms, in east wing in B Zone,
There's visits by a "caring" carer on phone
Who scores points for a top care home.

I want to buy something so number ring,
A foreign voice says, "Hi" - then they begin.
I want advice but can't get a word in;
They follow a script, and they are not listening.
What happened to Customer being King?
No thank you, box-ticking Singh!!

In town cars park, the ticket price is steep,
You can park a Vauxhall, Tesla, Mini or Jeep,
Be late by 3 mins and it won't be cheap,
A parking warden person will make you weep,
As they dish out fines to you naughty peeps!

Initiative is rare, everything is planned,
Corporate jobsworths just following commands.
No questioning the rules with corporate brands
Welcome all to Tick Box Land!!

March 2024

## The Dating Game

Ex wives, ex-husbands, ex trauma: post-divorce
Ex army, express relationships of course
There's saucy glampers, old hippies, glams,
Outdoor types craving cuddles in camper vans
On Big Fish, Adult Friends, and Silver Seniors:
Find love and lust you don't need to be a genius.
Skint gormless women accessed with a few clicks:
It's easy to find naïve over-trusting chicks.

So much choice to view on mad profiles,
Set a radius to your postcode in km or miles.
All these ex-marines and pilots with perfect smiles,
So many faces grace us in beguiling styles.

Abuse gets a block; a wink gets a view,
A bad report gets you locked so you can't get through.
The words on the profiles don't seem to be true
With profile pics dated in "properties" from '92.
It's all smoke and daggers, it's not tickety-boo
If you don't do psychology, you won't have a clue!

You got to select a partner who ain't naff,
Agree the day and date, then choose a gaff,
A cheap date in a bar, a pub or a caf'
And make sure you get your date to laugh
Cos listening and laughing are sure-fire hits,
You have to woo the brain and use your wits,
It's the path to get to the much naughtier bits
Like legs and thighs and chest and... hips.

It's all do-able courtesy of Plenty of Fish
Whatever build, body, colour or religion you wish
Just mind the bunny-boiling moms called Trish
Who'll be serving your pet up on a dish.

Blind dates, dinner dates, modest site subscription rates,
Post friend zoning, let's just be mates.
He was OK but weird, not so great,
An ego pump, needed to inflate.
You met, you crashed, now it's too late,
A merry-go-round of merry-making fakes.
The naked ape, sour grapes
No love lost, what a cost, time to vape,
Join the dating game; no time to wait!!

July 2023

## My Cabby And I

A Muslim cabby asked my view on God
(with a capital G which I find odd).
"MY... God," I said, "is like a giant tree...
It is you and it is me
And every atom and every planet afar,
Every galaxy, cluster and distant star,
Every Muslim, Sikh and Catholic Soul,
Everything is God for it is the whole.
Every smiling and crying woman and man
Is my God dear Mr Taxi Man.
Dawkins, Hawking, Darwin too
Are God and so are me and you."

My answer perplexed his scripted brain
Like a 'bot he asked me once again,
"Are you perhaps an atheist dude?
If you don't think that question rude?
For I wish to save my fellow man,
and teach what is taught in the Qur'an."

"You see this car I drive," says he
Well, it needs me at the wheel."
That was his allegorical way to say
God should be your driver, Neil.
"You cannot have a car without a maker,
You cannot have a man without a God.
For when your body's at the undertaker's
Your soul won't get the nod.
See even if you murder twenty-seven,
But believe in Allah and repent.
You will still go up to heaven,
And your free ticket will be sent."

"But what happens if I'm gay?" I say
In jest to check his thoughts.
"I like to spend weekends away
In fishnet vests & latex shorts."

"BISMILLAH! No place for queers
Change and save your soul.
Or face disgrace, pain and tears
In the devil's place below."

I point out that people are born this way,
Because God makes no mistakes.
At least it's what Lady Gaga says,
Yet he thinks such people flakes.
"They need to deny their physical self
And control earthly needs and desires."
For holiness is his only wealth
He needs the insurance for when he expires.

He said the Qur'an it detests, (to put it blunt),
LGBT and women's rights,
And the man in the front just sounds a cunt,
Yet he is blameless in his plight.
Because from being a bairn he was taught
The ways of a medieval Meccan prophet.
Taught to fear and not to have thought
By his family and church in profit.

Really, he is a good man I truly believe,
Despite staunch adoption of blind faith,
But I'm afraid it's sad and makes me grieve,
And a factor in why our world's not safe.

To him on high, to the main man he prays,
Through blind belief in some despotic creator
"Do you believe in God?" he says,
"No, I believe in something greater!"

March 2024

# Voice in the Forest

Amid the spruce and the pine and the larch and the fir
I was lost, I was missing my golden-locked girl.
I was wishing to be kissing, wishing she was there
Under the anarchy and canopy of the bold Douglas Fir.

The trees were so still under nimbostratus cloud
And echoes in the forest seemed to shout out loud.
"I'm here, help me!" a voice urgently cowed
Where Tortuosa Beach tortuously bowed.

Alarmed and lost and afraid of my plight
I hurriedly scurried through the dark and the bright,
Where the shadows cascaded demons in light
Towards the voice I hastened with all of my might.

The voice that I heard had got me quick to rail,
Heart pounding loud as I tried to prevail
Through the dark green evergreen, dieback in dale
Like a lost little puppy aimlessly chasing its tail.

No matter what I heard or feared, no matter where I ran,
I found evidence of nothing except the illusion of man.
The dreams to be found in a man's lifespan
Are like a conjuring trick or emails in spam.

Amid the spruce and the pine and the larch and the fir
Are just cones, and moans of wind in the air.
Despite a push and rush and a short little prayer
I realised for all that there is nobody there.

March 2024

## Jeanine

Your tummy was slim,
Your hips were wide,
You were not prim,
Yet had class and pride.
Your hair short and straight,
Eyes green like brine,
How I could relate
To my euro feline.

I thought out of my league
Such a perfect wench,
You were born in Liège
Spoke Walloon & French,
And English and German,
And a bit of Yorkshire too,
And I did determine
I really fancied you.

Oh, lady you woke me,
Thought you were the one,
You set my heart free
But we couldn't get on
Our souls were all lined up
But our behaviour all wrong.
We had a break up
And then I moved along.

*View From Here*

It is a long story
And I am not proud,
I am ultimately sorry
And my head is bowed.
We loved one another
So intense that it hurt,
There is such a story here lover
But this version is curt.

Because of you I learned that
I should follow my heart.
You were my love cat
And you were the start.
I followed my heart thus
And joy to me it thence came.
I hope you are well puss
And feel no malice or blame.

Learn your lessons with glory
And do not finger poke.
We all have our story
And one day we will croak.
Learn and love and be happy
No matter what else you do.
Don't be bitter or crabby,
Don't be remorseful or blue.
We all have our love drama
In our lives to relate.
Move on with your karma
And life can be great.

April 2024

BV - #0026 - 171024 - C4 - 229/152/9 - PB - 9781915657626 - Gloss Lamination